History Almost Forgotten

John & Esther VanBelle

Trilogy Christian Publishers

A Wholly Owned Subsidiary of Trinity Broadcasting Network

2442 Michelle Drive

Tustin, CA 92780

Copyright © 2024 by John & Esther VanBelle

All Scripture quotations, unless otherwise noted, taken from THE HOLY BIBLE, NEW INTERNATIONAL VERSION®, NIV® Copyright © 1973, 1978, 1984, 2011 by Biblica, Inc.® Used by permission. All rights reserved worldwide.

Scripture quotations marked (KJV) taken from *The Holy Bible, King James Version*. Cambridge Edition: 1769.

All rights reserved, including the right to reproduce this book or portions thereof in any form whatsoever.

For information, address Trilogy Christian Publishing

Rights Department, 2442 Michelle Drive, Tustin, CA 92780.

Trilogy Christian Publishing/ TBN and colophon are trademarks of Trinity Broadcasting Network.

For information about special discounts for bulk purchases, please contact Trilogy Christian Publishing.

Trilogy Disclaimer: The views and content expressed in this book are those of the author and may not necessarily reflect the views and doctrine of Trilogy Christian Publishing or the Trinity Broadcasting Network.

10 9 8 7 6 5 4 3 2 1

Library of Congress Cataloging-in-Publication Data is available.

B-ISBN#: 979-8-89041-487-8
E-ISBN#: 979-8-89041-488-5

Table of Contents

Chapter 1: Introduction 1

Chapter 2: In the Beginning 3

Chapter 3: European Influence 5

Chapter 4: Stained Glass Windows 8

Chapter 5: Church Bells 10

Chapter 6: Native American Religion in Northwest America 13

Chapter 7: The Black Robes 16

Chapter 8: St. Joseph Mission on the Ahtanum 1847 18

Chapter 9: Whitman Mission or the Mission at Waiilatpu, 1836 ...24

Chapter 10: St. Joachim's Mission Church Lummi Indian Reservation, Washington State, 1861 28

Chapter 11: Cataldo Mission, 1842, Cataldo, Idaho 33

Chapter 12: Indian Shaker Churches, Yakama Indian Nation, 1910 37

Chapter 13: St. Andrew's Episcopal Church, Chelan, Washington, 1897 41

Chapter 14: Little Stone Church, Chelan, Washington, 1890 45

Chapter 15: Mary Queen of Heaven Parish, Sprague, Washington, 1882 50

Chapter 16: History "Almost" Forgotten..54

Chapter 17: St. Michael's Episcopal Church Yakima, Washington, 1885..59

Chapter 18: Pioneer Presbyterian Church on Clatsop Plains, Warrington, Oregon, 1850 63

Chapter 19: The Church at Columbus Landing, Maryhill, Washington, 1888..70

Chapter 20: First Presbyterian Church, Bickleton, Washington, 1903..73

Chapter 21: Tualatin Plains Presbyterian Church, Old Scotch Church, 1873..78

Chapter 22: St Paul's Lutheran Church, Douglas, Washington, 1889..84

Chapter 23: St. James Episcopal Church, Cashmere, Washington 91

Chapter 24: Holy Trinity Temple Russian Orthodox Church, Wilkeson, Washington, 1896 95

Chapter 25: Visitation Catholic Church, Verboort Oregon,1875...99

Chapter 26: St. Joseph's Catholic Church, Waterville, Washington, 1892..104

Chapter 27: St. Peter's, The Dalles Oregon, 1848.......................107

Chapter 28: Coupeville United Methodist Church, Coupeville Washington...114

Chapter 29: Saint Joseph's Mission, Nez Perce Indian Reservation, 1874..118

Chapter 30: Saint Mary's Church, White Swan, Washington, 1887 121

Chapter 31: The Cathedral of Our Lady of Lourdes, Spokane, Washington, 1881..124

Chapter 32: Immaculate Conception Church, Roslyn, Washington, 1888..127

Chapter 33: First Congregational Church, Coupeville Washington,1889...132

Chapter 34: Holy Trinity Episcopal Church, Wallace Idaho, 1910 134

Chapter 35: Mount Pisgah Presbyterian Church, Roslyn Washington, 1886...138

Chapter 36: Seventh - Day Adventists Church, Walla Walla, Washington, 1874...143

Chapter 37: Old St. Peter's Episcopal Church, Tacoma, Washington, 1873...146

Chapter 38: Bethel African Methodist Episcopal Church, Yakima Washington, 1906...150

Memorial

This book is a memorial to Esther, my wife, partner, and co-author of this publication.

Esther went to be with the Lord on July 20, 2018. Her passing was a spiritual journey for the family and her friends at Quail Run in Terrace Heights, an active adult community where she was instrumental in starting a women's prayer meeting called Care, Share and Prayer. In 1985, she joined Open Doors with Brother Andrew, also known as God's smugglers. She was involved in putting on banquets and making presentations to raise funds to purchase Bibles for Russia and Romania.

For six years, she prayer walked around City Hall and County Courthouse each week and prayed with the homeless. She volunteered at the Union Gospel Mission, Life Choices. Many people were touched by her cards of support and encouragement.

Her works for the kingdom of God are too many to mention, but we know that the greeting she received was "Well done, thou good and faithful servant."

Acknowledgements

I want to thank my wife Esther for joining me in this endeavor and the encouragement not to give up.

Thank you to my grandson, Trenton Bickel, and my son, Larry VanBelle, for their technical input to make this possible.

I also want to thank all the members of the different churches who were willing to provide the information that is included in this book.

In memory of my wife Esther.
1930-2018
The co-author of this manuscript.

Proceeds received from this book above the cost of printing will be donated to Habitat for Humanity

Chapter 1

Introduction

Why this book? Why write a book about church history? The main purpose is to preserve the rich history of the development and the growth of the places of worship in the Northwest.

Since the beginning of time, men worshipped a supreme being. It is our intent to document the development of religion and the spread of the Gospel throughout the region.

Our research covers three main interests:

Historians—persons interested in the historic development of a segment of society that is not well known.

Theologians—how and when the settlers began to worship at a certain location.

Architects and designers—in the construction of the early buildings used for worship, many interesting designs were used.

The geographic area covered by this research is the Northwest, including the states of Idaho, Oregon, and Washington.

In most cases the stories as written are exact duplications of the information provided by the churches, in order to capture the flavor of the people attending that church.

Some information was obtained, with permission, from museums and newspaper clippings provided by local historians.

The Ahtanum Mission with the Tipi donated by the Yakamas.

It is our hope and prayer that this book will again reinforce our belief that the church will be here until the end of time, and the words spoken by our Lord to Peter that,

"The gates of hell will not prevail against it".

The places of worship did not begin with the coming of the white settlers.

Well before the arrival of the "Black Robes," religious practices took place among the natives which were an important part of their culture. The Native American way of worship will be covered in one of the first chapters.

Chapter 2

In the Beginning

Since the beginning of time, humans have had a desire to worship a being larger than themselves. Adam and Eve worshipped the creator God in the garden of Eden. Jews worship the same God today. Muslims worship Allah. Many Native American tribes worship the Creator God during the Feast of the First Fruit each year.

From this point on, we find many different variations in worship and understanding of God, who created the heavens and the earth. From early history we learn that the first place of worship was the outdoors. Adam and Eve communicated with God in the cool of the evening. Later, altars were erected as places of worship. They were made of stones from the fields and could not be shaped or hewn by men.

As time went on, the location of worship changed from being the outdoor altar to a tent, also called a tabernacle. Since many early peoples were nomads, tents could be moved very easily from location to location. The Hebrew people were in the dessert for 40 years, so a tabernacle that could be quickly moved from place to place, was the ideal place of worship.

As society became more stable and people stayed in one location, temples were constructed: the most notable by King Solomon. This temple was made from stones and cedar, overlaid with gold and precious stones.

It was not very long before the focus of worship became many gods. These gods came in a multitude of different forms. Many were made from wood or stone and were made to fit the imagination of the worshipper.

Garden of the Gods, Colorado Springs Colorado.

As we can see, the places and methods of worship have changed throughout history. It began with worshipping in nature and at the altar to within a tent and/or a building. Today the places of worship have many different names, from cathedral, to synagogue, to mosque, to church, temple, and many others.

Chapter 3
European Influence

When traveling Europe, it is impossible not to see the beautiful cathedrals and churches. They were constructed in different time frames and by different architects, but at the same time they have many of the same characteristics.

Most of the great cathedrals were constructed between the 12th and the 15th centuries. The first being in France, Germany, England, Italy, Holland, and Belgium. Several of the cathedrals in America are copies of the original European cathedrals.

The most prominent type of architecture is the Gothic style, which was developed in the Middle Ages. This is often called the flamboyant style and can be identified by its pointed arches.

To build a cathedral, stone carvers, carpenters, masons, architect, laborers, blacksmiths, roofers, glassmakers, stained glass craftsmen and sculptors were needed. Building a building like the cathedral could take hundreds of years. The trades were handed down from father to son. Next to the architect, the stone masons were the most important craftsmen as the stones had to be precisely cut and placed in the foundation.

The roof was the only part of the structure made of wood; oak was preferred for this job. Plumbers overlaid the roof with lead or slate tiles. According to some historians, the height of the roof was determined by the height necessary to keep fire from reaching the roof. Gutters were added to draw rainwater away from the building. At the corners of the roof, where the gutters joined together, gargoyles were used to keep the water away from the foundation. These often-resembled heads of animals or church leaders.

The massive walls were made with stones from the local quarry. They had to be precisely cut and put into place with mortar. The windows were tall and narrow in the Gothic style so as not to weaken the wall as it had to support the massive roof. Openings such as windows and doors would reduce the load bearing ability.

Piazza Santa Croce and Façade of the Church Florence, Italy

Flying buttresses prevented the walls from leaning outward under the weight of the roof system. The buttresses were outside the structure, from the top of the wall to the ground. The most impressive ones are at the Notre Dame cathedral in France.

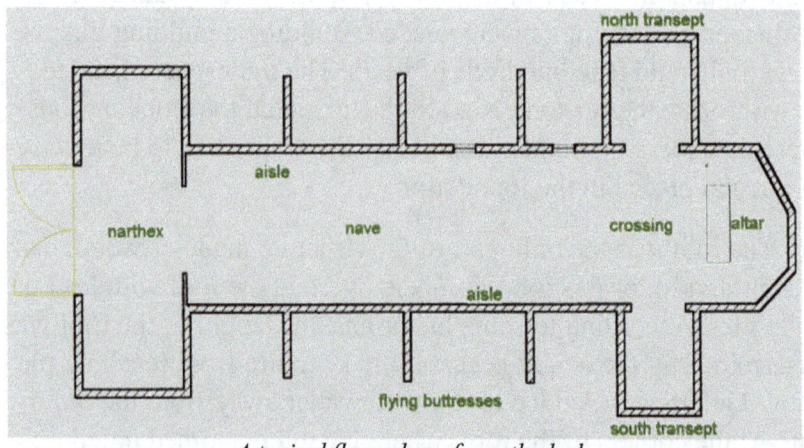

A typical floor plan of a cathedral.

In general, the floor plan of most cathedrals is in the shape of the cross. In many European churches, the altar is at the east end. This design was brought to many of the New World churches. Prominent persons from the community were buried beneath the floor. According to Scripture, when Jesus returns, He will come in the eastern sky. (On that day, the resurrection will take place.) It has been the custom throughout the ages to bury people with the head towards the west so that when the resurrection takes place, they will be facing east. For the same reason, worshippers in many churches today sit in pews facing east.

The south wall was designed with more windows than the north wall. The north wall is called the Old Testament Wall and the south the New Testament Wall. The New Testament proclaims Jesus as the light of the world that is the reason for bringing more light through the south wall. Another factor is that in Europe, being in the northern hemisphere, more light will enter the building from the south. Few windows in the north wall will keep the cold northern winds from entering the building through poorly insulated windows.

Stained glass windows were installed to explain the gospel to the people attending services. The mass was difficult to understand since it was done in Latin, and many members were illiterate. Bibles were not readily available to lay persons, and if they were, most people were not able to read them.

Chapter 4

Stained Glass Windows

In researching the history of the early churches in the Northwest, we found that placing a stained-glass window in the church was very important. In most cases, the window was donated by a prominent church member or a church group, such as a women's society.

The earliest examples of windows with figurative scenes are at St. Remi in Reims, France from around the year 1000 A.D. Not many colors were available in the early days of cathedral construction. These colors were saffron-yellow, purplish-red, green-blue, and copper-red. After 1300 A.D., other colors came into use, such as light-yellow and reddish-yellow. These colors were added into the glass.

The artist cuts the glass and places it together with H-shaped strips of lead, called calms. Cracks between the glass and lead are filled with putty to make the window waterproof.

In the late 1200s, more and more glass-window spaces were used in the great cathedrals of France. This form of decoration of churches was followed by the cathedrals in Germany and England. Through the 1500s, the demand for stained-glass windows continued, but the artists began using flesh tones and softer colors. However, it is sad that the colors soon faded.

Several churches in our Northwest have stained glass windows made by the famous artist Joseph Povey. Mr. Povey emigrated from England to the United States in 1848. In England, his family for generations had been trained in the art of making stained glass windows. Here in the US, the business prospered, and in 1890, other family members moved to Portland, Oregon to work in his studio.

St. Michael's Church in Yakima, WA.

Povey windows can be found in Dallas at the Old St. Paul's Episcopal Diocesan Chapel, the Corvallis Christian church, and others.

Chapter 5
Church Bells

For centuries, the church bell played an important role in everyday life. It called the faithful to worship and announced the passing of the same. Before the invention of the clock, it was used to tell time. The church bell was also used as a call to prayer in the evening; this was called the Angelus. The workers working in the fields would hear the bell toll and knew that it was time to retire, go home, and say their prayers.

As early as the year 400 A.D. bells were installed in churches and were first introduced in the town of Campania, in Italy. The bells were used to call the faithful to worship but also to give the alarm when danger threatened.

As time went on, towers were constructed on churches to carry the sound of the bell throughout the surrounding area. This became more important when clocks were designed and installed in the towers. Many church bells were engraved with appropriate inscriptions.

In England, they often used quaint verses. The following is typical:

> *Men's death I tell by doleful knell;*
> *Lightning and thunder I break asunder;*
> *On Sabbath all to church I call;*
> *The sleepy head I rouse from bed;*
> *The tempest's rage I do assuage;*
> *When cometh harm, I sound alarm.*

Typical Church Bell

The material used to make a bell is called bell metal. It is a mixture of copper and tin. During the second World War, several of the bells were removed from the churches in the German occupied countries. The bell from the church in my hometown of Ridderkerk was removed and put on a barge to be shipped to Germany. It was scheduled to be melted down and the material used for the German war effort. The barge was spotted by an Allied airplane and was sunk. After the war, the barge was raised, and the bell identified and placed back in the tower. It has worked every hour and half hour to tell the time and call the faithful to worship on Sunday ever since.

Some bells are made with two clappers, one big one in the center to call the faithful to worship and one mounted on the outside of the bell to create a different sound used to inform the community about disasters.

History Almost Forgotten

Church at Ridderkerk Holland

Chapter 6

Native American Religion in Northwest America

Many books are written about the religions of the American natives. The religious practices differ from tribe to tribe. Common practices are found among tribes that resided in the same geographic area.

A.J. Splawn in his book, *Ka-mi-akin, the Last Hero of the Yakimas*, gives a detailed account of the Indian history in central Washington.

To fully understand the Native religions, we have to accept the fact that they do not distinguish between the natural and the supernatural. They perceive the "material" and "spiritual" to be of the same realm. Since they lived close to nature and made that a big part of their religion, it did vary from tribe to tribe. Some of the coastal Indians concentrated on whaling, while for the interior Indians, salmon was their main food and part of their religious feasts.

The authors had the privilege to be invited to the "Feast of the First Fruit" by the Yakamas. The ceremony was held in the Satus longhouse. The men were seated on one side of the building while the women were on the other side. The drummers were at the end of the building away from the kitchen. The drummers would drum a prayer for water, salmon, venison, and roots. Between prayers we partook of a small portion of each. This was followed by a feast of plenty. Any food remaining was taken to the elderly and sick of the tribe.

One predominant religion among many of the Northwestern tribes was the Dreamer religion.

It is believed that it originated with the Wi-nah-pams or Priest Rapids Indians.

Tradition has it that So-wap-so erected a pole in front of his lodge. On this pole, he would receive messages from the Great Spirit, written on buckskin foretelling the future of the tribe. Using this method, he was able to foretell the coming of the white man many years before they arrived.

St. Joachim's Mission Church

The first white men passed through; while the second group build houses and exchange things for skins of animals.

After these came the white men who will tell you about the white men's God. They will be wearing black robes.

Next, and last will come the white men who will overrun the red men's country. The hunting grounds will be no more, and the roots and berries will disappear. This information was passed on to his son, who gave it to his wife for safe keeping when they went berry picking. She placed it under a rock and then forgot what rock she placed it under. As far as we can research, most tribes believed in life after death. They believed in a Creator God and in a bad spirit called Lucifer.

Chapter 7

The Black Robes

It was in March 1831 that four Indians traveled to St. Louis to see General William Clark. Three were from the Nez Perce tribe and one was from the Flathead tribe. The purpose of the trip was to find out more about the white man and seek the "white men's book of heaven."

William Walker, a half-breed Wyandotte who had been converted to Christianity, learned about this journey by the Natives and wrote a letter to a New York businessman.

This letter was well received and was published in a widely read newspaper. This generated an almost immediate response.

The Roman Catholic priests were the first missionaries to the Northwest and, because of the robes they wore, were called Black Robes.

In most cases, the priests were well received. The priests were mission driven with a desire to help the natives. Their simplistic lifestyle and humility were admired by the natives.

They believed in the words spoken by Francis of Assisi many years ago, who said, "Go and spread the Gospel and use words if you have to."

After the first priests, missionaries with different ideas and focus came. Their focus was the making of converts instead of helping the natives. This was very confusing to the natives as they were forced into a different lifestyle.

The Rev. Father F. N. Blanchet made first use of this Catholic ladder in July of 1842 at the Cowlitz mission (also known as St. Francis Mission) in order to teach the natives the truth of the Catholic faith. Many copies of the ladder were made and presented to the Indian chiefs; thereafter, it was in constant use among the Northwest Indians. A display featuring the Catholic Ladder stands on the grounds of St. Francis Mission. The 40 horizontal bars represent the 40 centuries B.C. The 33 bars represent the years of Christ's life on earth. Noah's ark and the 10 Commandments are shown with the star of Bethlehem and Joseph, Mary and Jesus.

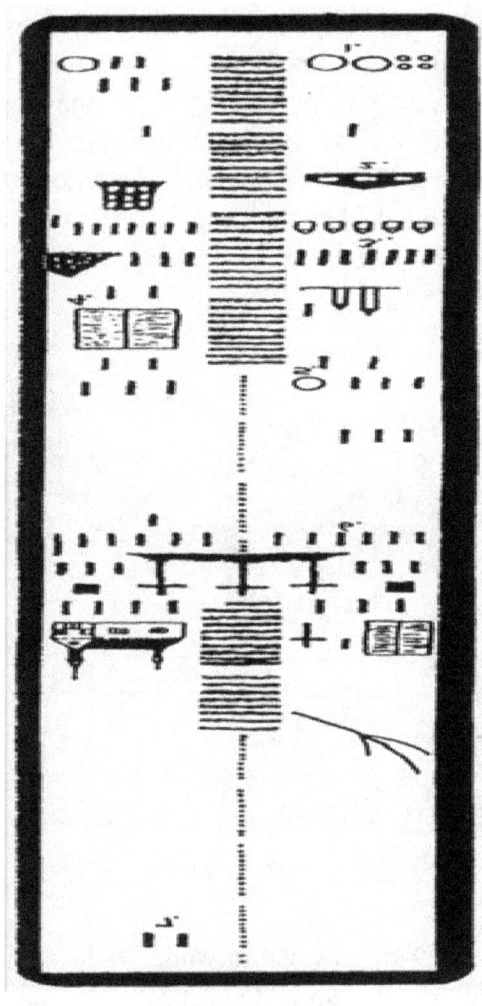

The Catholic Ladder.

Chapter 8

St. Joseph Mission on the Ahtanum 1847

From the archives of the Ahtanum Mission with permission.

Charles Pandosy and Eugene C. Chirouse left France with a desire to be missionaries to the Indians of the Pacific Northwest. Their first stop was in Quebec, Canada, where they joined Bishop A.M.A. Blanchet in 1847 and then traveled across America to the Oregon Territory. They were the first priests to be ordained in the State of Washington (then the Oregon Territory) in January of 1848.

The Rectory, home of the priests.

Yakima Chief Owhi traveled to Walla Walla and asked Bishop Blanchet to send "Black Robes" to his people so they could learn the Christian faith. He gave them land for their first missions and provided them with his protection.

Five missions in all were established in the Yakama country, from 1847 to 1852.

The first was St. Rose, near the headwaters of the Yakima River. Second, the Immaculate Conception near Manastash creek, a few miles from Ellensburg. Third was St Joseph in the Simcoe area, near the present town of White Swan. Fourth was Holy Cross near Moxee. Fifth, St. Joseph mission in the Ahtanum Valley.

In the fall of 1852, Fathers Pandosy and Louis D'Herbomez were asked by Chief Kamiakin to establish a mission on his land to minister to his people. They chose the present site for the mission located next to the Ahtanum creek in the Upper Yakima Valley.

During the spring of 1853, work on the new mission began.

Father Pandosy and Chirouse are credited for having been the first in the state of Washington to use the technique of irrigation, which they taught to the Yakamas.

Chief Kamiakin loved to garden. He would share his vegetables with the priests and provided them with meat during the winter months.

The poverty of the priests was so severe that their clothing consisted only of tattered robes. On one occasion, Father Pandosy walked on his bare feet from Ellensburg to Walla Walla to report to Bishop Blanchet.

These priests were the first non-Indians to reside in the Yakima country.

(*Note: the name of the city of Yakima and the name of Yakima County are spelled differently than the official name of the tribe and bands that make up the Yakama Nation.*)

A visitor to the Mission in 1853 Theodore Winthrop, wrote the following in his book, *Canoe and Saddle*:

Present sign at the Mission.

"As I drew near, a sound of reverent voices met me, vespers in this station in the wilderness...But a sense of the divine presence was there, not less than in many dim old cathedrals...where prayer had made its home for centuries, has prayer seemed as mighty, worship so near the ear of God, as vespers here at his rough shrine in the lonely valley of the Atinam."

St Joseph (Ahtanum) Mission.

The priests were present for and signed the Walla Walla Treaty in 1855.

In October of 1855, the local Indian Wars broke out. Following the battle at Union Gap on November 14, 1855, the U.S Army and the Oregon volunteers moved onto the mission property. Father Pandosy and Paul Durieu fled for their lives, taking several Catholic Yakamas with them. After fourteen days of little sleep and no food, they arrived at the Jesuit Mission in Colville.

The Alter as it is today

Lt. Philip H. Sheridan, who later rose to rank of general in the Civil War, was present at the mission on that day and wrote in his memoirs the following:

> **While Nesmith was looking for Capt. Maurice Malony's detachment, idle Volunteers and Regulars looted the mission, rifled caches around the property. Men paraded derisively investments taken from the church, Regulars burglarized the buildings, vegetables, and flour, sacramental. wine, a half keg of gunpowder and whatever was moveable were stolen, divided up or destroyed. The mission was reduced to ashes by a deliberately set fire that climaxed the frolic. November 14, 1855. They were more convincing as common pillagers than brave Indian fighters.**

The rebuilding of the Mission began in the spring of 1868. Father Louis St. Onge traveled into the woods near Tampico to cut the logs and pulled them to this location.

With the help of some Yakamas, they hand hewed the logs and put them into place.

Typical log construction at the Ahtanum Rectory

The timber in the Tampico area is mostly white fir and some ponderosa pine.

Log buildings built by generations before us were important symbols of our American history. A log cabin was the birthplace of Abraham Lincoln, as well as other national figures.

Log construction was not invented in the United States but brought here by settlers from Northwest and Central Europe. Wood selection was mostly determined by the availability, but the hardest type of wood was used for the foundation.

Horizontal spaces or joints between the logs were usually filled with a combination of materials that together is known as chinking. First, a dry, bulky, rigid blocking, such as wood slabs or stones were inserted into the joints, followed by soft packing material such as moss, clay, or dried animal dung.

The Ahanum Mission was completed in 1870 and dedicated by Bishop Blanchett on July 15, 1872.

The mission stood alone, deserted until the early 1900s when the Knights of Columbus raised funds and purchased the land from squatters who had taken possession of it. The buildings were placed on foundations, the logs re-chinked, and the roof replaced.

The mission was placed on the National Historic Register in 1977.

Chapter 9

Whitman Mission or the Mission at Waiilatpu, 1836

This information is from the information available at the site, with permission from the National Park Service.

Waiilatpu, meaning "place of the people of the rye grass," is the site of a mission founded in 1836 among the Cayuse Indians by Marcus and Narcissa Whitman.

Covered wagon on the Historic Route of the Oregon Trail.

As immigrants began moving across the continent into the Pacific Northwest during the 1840s, the mission also became an important station of the Oregon Trail.

Stirred by accounts of explorers and traders, missionaries had become interested in the Oregon country in the 1820s, but the remoteness of the area discouraged them.

In 1833, an article in a New York Methodist publication described the visit of western Indians seeking teachers and the white man's "Book of Heaven" (the Bible). Although this story was mostly fictional, it stimulated missionary interest.

In 1835, the American Board of Foreign Missions, representing several Protestant churches, sent the Rev. Samuel Parker and Dr. Marcus Whitman to the Oregon country to select mission sites. On the way, the men talked to some Indians at a fur traders' rendezvous and became convinced that the prospects were good.

To save time, Parker continued to explore Oregon for sites, and Whitman returned east to recruit more workers. Soon, the Rev. Henry Spalding and his wife, Eliza, William Gray, and Narcissa Prentiss, whom Whitman married on February 18, 1836, were headed westward in covered wagons.

The journey was a notable one in the story of the Oregon Trail. Narcissa Whitman and Eliza Spalding were the first white women to cross the continent overland, and the missionary wagon, reduced to a cart, was the first vehicle to travel as far west as Fort Boise. Their successful trek inspired many families to follow.

Other mission societies were already active in Oregon. In 1834, Methodists under Jason Lee began work in the Willamette Valley. Later, Catholic missions were established along the lower Columbia.

The Whitmans opened their mission among the Cayuse at Waiilatpu and the Spaldings among the Nez Perce at Lapwai. The missionaries learned the Indian languages and assigned the words into English spellings. Spalding printed books in Nez Perce and Spokane on a press brought to Lapwai in 1839.

From the book Whitman Mission *by Erwin N. Thompson*

Progress in spiritual matters was slow. The Indians were indifferent to religious worship, books, and school. In 1842, reports of dissension and the lack of funds caused the board to order the Waiilatpu and Lapwai stations closed. Convinced that the missions should stay open, Whitman undertook a remarkable overland journey in mid-winter to plead his case personally with the board. The board, moved by his arguments, rescinded its orders.

After 11 years of working with the Indians, the mission effort ended in violence. There were several causes behind the Indian unrest. Deep cultural differences between the white and the Indian ways of life had caused tension and misunderstanding. Increased numbers of immigrants and stories of settlers taking Indian land elsewhere convinced the Cayuse that their way of life was in danger. A measles epidemic, brought in 1847 by the immigrants, spread rapidly among the Cayuse, who had no resistance to the disease, and within a short time half the tribe died.

When Whitman's medicine helped white children but not theirs, many Cayuses believed they were being poisoned to make way for the immigrants.

On November 29, 1847, a band of Cayuse attacked the mission and killed Marcus Whitman, his wife, the Sager boys, and nine others. A few survivors escaped, but 50, mostly women and children, were taken captive.

Three children died from the measles, and the others were ransomed a month later by Peter Skene Ogden of the Hudson Bay Company. The killings ended Protestant missions in the Oregon country and led to war against the Cayuse by settlers from the Willamette and lower Columbia Valleys.

In 1848, Joseph Meek carried news of the tragedy and petitions from the settlers to Congress. Congress created the Oregon Territory in August of that year, the first formal territorial government west of the Rockies. A memorial monument was constructed in 1897 on the 50th anniversary of the Whitmans' deaths.

Memorial Monument, which is 27 feet high.

Chapter 10

St. Joachim's Mission Church Lummi Indian Reservation, Washington State, 1861

Information from the archives of the Center for Pacific Northwest Studies Western Washington University. Bellingham, Washington.

Sir Francis Drake claimed to have reached latitude 48 in 1579, about the latitude of Everett, Washington. A Greek mariner known as Juan de Fuca, claimed to have sailed and entered a broad sea inlet in 1592. Captain Vancouver sent Joseph Whidby to explore the straits in 1782. South of Birch Bay, explorers and surveyors found the Lummi Indians.

The history of the Lummis is very colorful, with incidents of much interest, but as the personalities making history were illiterate, nearly all sources of historical information have sunk into the grave along with their actors.

According to the statements obtained from the still living old Lummi Indians, the land occupied by the Lummis at present were always the most chosen by their forefathers. When chief Selome held sway among the Lummis, all villages of the Nooksack Valley paid tribute to that chief.

White settlers started moving into the region at the turn of the 19th century. Canadian travelers followed the Lewis and Clark expeditions in 1804 and 1805. Many of the Canadians were of the Roman Catholic faith.

Lummis became acquainted with Fr. Chirouse while he was at Tulalip during their frequent visits for religious instructions. In 1860, Fr. Chirouse paid the first visit to them, and in 1861 with the help of the Lummis, he built the little log chapel dedicated to St. Joachim near the mouth of the Nooksack river. St Joachim is assumed to be the father of Mary, the mother of Jesus.

Fr. E. Casimir Chirouse was born in the town of Bourge de Peage in a pleasant valley about fifty miles from Lyons in France on May 8, 1821.

After he read a letter about the conditions among the Northwest Indian population west of the Cascade mountains, the young Chirouse was greatly impressed. At the age of 15, he made up his mind to become a priest and missionary to reach the Indians in the northwest of the United States. He arrived in New York on April 2, 1847 with other priests, and they began their journey west.

The priests began their work among the Cayuse, Yakama, and Kittitas Indians.
The St Anne's chapel among the Cayuse was opened on November 27, 1847. This was short lived, for two days later the Whitman massacre took place and the priests from this location were forced to seek refuge at the Dalles. Fr. Chirouse worked among the Yakamas and was instrumental in the construction of the St. Rose mission.

This dugout canoe is located adjacent to the church.

In 1867, farmer C.C Finkbonner oversaw the Lummi Reservation.

Bishop Blanchett in a letter to Gen. McKenny praises the harmony between the priests and Mr. Finkbonner. In the same letter, he mentions that there are 40 good houses for the Indians and a little church that will be very nice when it is finished.

The Lummis were always friendly to the white settlers; this was not always appreciated by the settlers. Many Indians lived off the reservation. They objected to being returned to the reservation. Today, this church is a thriving community, and a large group of members are attending mass on Saturday evening.

Interior of the church.

History Almost Forgotten

Church exterior

Chapter 11

Cataldo Mission, 1842, Cataldo, Idaho

Information obtained from the Visitor's Guide with permission.

Before the first white men began entering the land, a tribe of Indians lived along the shores of Lake Coeur d'Alene and the surrounding territory.

The Old Cataldo Mission Idaho

They were a proud people, peaceful, intelligent, and attractive. They lived in Tipis and moved throughout this area in search of game, fish, berries, and roots.

The tribe of 2,500 to 4,000 Indians were originally called the "Schee-chu-umsh" of "Schistu-umsh." They were renamed the

Coeur d'Alene Indians, meaning "heart of the awl," by French trappers who considered them shrewd bargainers.

The Coeur d'Alenes were very spiritual, and when they heard that a neighboring tribe had a "medicine man" of great powers, they decided they wanted this magic for themselves.

They sent out word that the "Black Robes," Catholic Jesuit priests, would be welcomed among their people. So, in the early 1840s Jesuit missionaries came into north Idaho.

THE OLD MISSION rose like a miracle in almost total wilderness, where even log houses were rare.

The mission measures about 90 feet high and 40 feet wide. The 6 square, upright timbers in front are 28 inches square and the two by the altar are 3 feet by 3 feet. All are more than 25 feet long and were hewn and planed with a broad ax. About midway between floor and ceiling, you can see where the horizontal timbers were mortised into uprights.

The altar as it now exists.

Here the wood pegs are also visible. Wooden pegs were used throughout the building to secure all structural members together. Some wooden pegs remain in the floor in the vicinity of the altar.

The two paintings above the side altars depicting Heaven and Hell are Old World works of art and were transported to the wilderness by Black Robes.

Antonio Ravalli, born May 16, 1812, in Ferrara, Italy, entered the Society of Jesus November 12, 1827. Ordained as a priest in 1843, he joined Father Pierr-Jean Desmet's party of missionaries, and came to the Pacific Northwest.

Father Joseph Cataldo opened Saint Michael's Mission at Spokane in 1867.

The altar is the work of Father Ravalli, carved by hand and painted to achieve the effect of marble.

Father Ravalli designed the building in the tradition of the grand cathedrals of his birthplace. Ravalli was a Renaissance man.

He built the mission from sophisticated plans, using simple tools and untrained labor. The dome of the mission was one of several elements that created a grandeur and elegance reminiscent of the churches of Europe.

Fabric from the Hudson Bay Trading Post, purchased at Fort Walla Walla, was used on the interior walls. Chandeliers, designed to replicate those found in the grand cathedrals in Italy were fashioned out of used tin cans. Wooden altars were painted and treated to resemble marble. In 1865, exterior siding and interior paneling, both made from local materials, were added to the building.

Massive, hewed beams are mortised and tenoned and all structural members are secured by wooden pegs. Holes were drilled in upright timbers and rafters; horizontal dowels were inserted between the uprights. The building was built using large logs cut at the site, then latticed with saplings that were woven with grass and caked with mud. The process was called wattle and daub.

The only tools Ravalli had were a broad axe, auger, ropes and pulleys, a pen knife, and an improvised whip saw.

The mission was fashioned in the architectural style known in America as Greek Revival. The building is 90 feet by 40 feet on a 4 feet wide foundation. The walls are a foot thick and hollow inside.

Under the leadership of Bishop Kelly, the support of many organizations in the Silver Valley, and the Inland Empire, the Old Mission Church was initially restored in 1928-1930. The foundation was strengthened, the floor made firm, the façade repaired, and the whole exterior painted white.

In 1973-76, the state of Idaho undertook the complete restoration of the church as a bicentennial project, spending $310,000.

Chapter 12

Indian Shaker Churches, Yakama Indian Nation, 1910

White Swan Shaker Church

    The Indians of Oregon first became acquainted with the Shaker religion through the influence of Kelso Shaker, known as Aiyel, and his followers in this area. The time was probably 1893. But officially this religion had its beginning in the winter of 1882-83 with the visions of John Slocum. Indian shakers believe that their religion is an instrument of God to provide relief to Indians in their time of need.

In 1882, John Slocum (Squ-sacht-um), a southern coast Salish Indian of the Squaxin group, was living near Olympia. According to the Shaker traditions, in that same year Slocum fell ill and died. While he was being prepared for his burial, he revived and announced his salvation.

He told his people that he had seen God and His angels. He was told he was wicked and must change his ways to enter heaven. According to the angels, the Indians needed to quit gambling, drinking, and smoking. He directed his followers to construct a church, and for several months, he preached salvation. However, many of his followers left the faith, and after four months, he returned to his "wicked" ways.

A year later, he became ill again, and it appeared that he would die. The medicine man was brought in, but this angered Slocum's wife Mary, and she left the house in protest.

While she was praying, she began to shake uncontrollably and could not stop shaking. She returned to the house and continued to pray over her husband as the shaking intensified. John Slocum recovered again; this was evidence to the Shaker community of God's medicine.

The Satus Shaker Church outside Granger, Washington.

News of this event spread like wildfire through the Indian communities. The greatest addition of converts to the new religion was among the Yakamas.

In 1890, the Shaker religion was introduced to the Yakama Nation by the Cowlitz and spread rapidly. The Yakamas in turn sent out missionaries to other tribes in Oregon and California. As in many Protestant churches, disputes continued to plague the church. A meeting in Yakima gave birth in 1953 to the Independent Shaker

Church. As with the Indian Full Gospel Church, the Yakima church advocated the use of the Bible in ritual.

The main entryway to the church sanctuary is opposite to the location of the steeple at both Shaker churches documented. In most churches, the main entry way is at the steeple.

Chapter 13

St. Andrew's Episcopal Church, Chelan, Washington, 1897

Information with permission from Rev. Melinda. St. Clair

    St Andrew's Episcopal Church is believed to be the oldest log church in the State of Washington that can claim an uninterrupted record of worship service by a single congregation.

    The church building remains very much the same today as it was when constructed nearly a century ago. In 1992, the church was recognized for its historical significance by being selected to the national Registry of Historic Places.

    The Lake Chelan area in the late 1800s consisted of a few dozen pioneers who were led to the area primarily by visions of great mineral wealth in the surrounding mountains and by the pristine beauty of the lake and the surrounding mountains. The local newspapers, *The Chelan Falls Leader,* carried regular articles recounting the anticipated finds of gold and silver (and even diamonds) awaiting discovery.

Chelan Falls with its location next to the Columbia River, was predicted to become the hub of central Washington. A mine-to-market rail link was expected to join the head of Lake Chelan to the Pacific Ocean. It was a time for dreams and visions.

One of these visions was to build an Episcopal church, and in 1889, a small group of church members gathered to plan and organize construction of a church building. Services at that time were held in homes and the schoolhouse.

Land for the church was procured on a portion of the Hewitt family homestead, and church members set up a logging camp along the south shore of the lake to cut logs for the building.

Stained glass windows in the back of the sanctuary.

The logs were towed down lake and stored near a sawmill in Lakeside, where they were left to season over a two-year period.

It was Captain Watkins on the steamer "Stehekin" who towed the logs down the lake. Bill Hern, with great strength and a team of horses, brought the logs down to the shore. Bill Hern was remembered to have said about the Rev. Brian Roberts, the vicar: "He is a pretty good cuss, so I will help him some to build his church."

The foundation cornerstone was laid in April 1897, and the peeled logs were hauled the two miles from Lakeside to the church site. In October 1898, a determined effort was begun to enclose the church before winter, and a crew of volunteers began installing the roof beams. The building was enclosed by December, allowing the first communion service to be held on Christmas Eve. Pews were not installed until the next month. The bell tower was completed in spring of 1899.

The design for the church is believed to have been the work of Kirtland Kelsey Cutter, a well-known and highly regarded architect from Spokane. (He was also recommended for having designed many classical structures, including the Idaho Pavilion at the 1893 Chicago World's Fair.). The main church building is a rectangle, measuring 25 feet on the north and south walls by 50 feet east and west. The base of the 40-foot-high bell tower forms the narthex, which is a 10 by 10 feet square.

The bell tower

The log walls are Douglas fir, milled on the top and the bottom and precisely notched to fit together without the need for chinking or other filler. The foundation is of local granite. The original multi-panel frosted glass windows have been replaced by still-present stained-glass windows with their religious themes. The only other significant changes from the original configuration are the additions of central heating to replace the original wood stove and the electric lighting.

The bell has the following inscription:

"To the Glory of God and in the loving memory of Mary W. Quirk. Born Dec.15, 1817, died Jan. 9, 1898. Born and died in the city of New York."

Excerpt from the Chelan Leader newspaper.

August 20, 1897. Fred Pflaeging who has been engaged in peeling the logs for the Episcopal church building began work on the stone foundation this week.

C. E. Whaley's black colt showed religious tendencies...walked into M. E. Sunday School last Sunday... proceeded leisurely up the aisle and would have joined the Bible class, but someone hustled him out of the door.

Spring 1988

Chapter 14

Little Stone Church, Chelan, Washington, 1890

The following is a presentation given at the 100th anniversary, November 23, 2003:

> The founders of this church were part of the great expansion into the western frontier of the United States. Simple folks who, for one reason or another, chose to come to live on the shores of Lake Chelan. It was here, with all the hardships of daily life, that they also undertook to educate their young in the ways of the Lord. And here too they sought assemblage to offer up praise and worship to their creator, their God.
>
> In 2003, we assembled in that church, bound together with Christian brothers and sisters of history, as tightly as with our friends sitting next to us today. These ties that bind are cords of Christ. And we, who gathered in joyful jubilee, celebrated 100 continuous years of existence and service, called these cords the Little Stone Church.

The Little Stone Church. Our church. Look at it! Much of our history is based on this room. It is as though God has used these four stone walls to shape us and define us as a church. We are not the "Big Stone Church," a factor that we deal with today. This building is a bit more rectangular than square, made of earth, wood, and stone. We organized as a church in 1890, but we mark from when this building was dedicated, December 13, 1903.

It was and still is held together by sweat and toil, mixed through and through with the love that people have for God and for each other. It was not and is not an opulent looking structure, either from without or within. But this simplistic, stately form for one hundred years has stood tall, beckoning out to a passing world that God and the simple people that serve Him can be found here.

John & Esther VanBelle

The church members dressed for the ocassion.

What God has done through the lives of the people He has brought here, intersecting them in crucial ways to shape our world, is what our history is all about. God, building His church through people. That is what we celebrate here today!

So, until the Lord returns, may our prayers be that His spirit continues to guide us and bind us as a family and as a church.

In 1889, Rev. Samuel Greene of the Agency of the Congregational Sunday School and Publishing Society at Chicago provided a guiding hand between 1889 and 1903. He was instrumental to get the church organized and in providing Sunday school material. Services were first held on a platform at the shores of Lake Chelan.

Today, new members are baptized in the lake during the summer months.

Looking over the list of pastors who served the congregation since the church was organized, it is typical of many churches' starts in the Northwest. Most pastors served only a few years before moving on to new locations.

On August 18, 1890, the First Congregational Church was organized, and in 1941, the property was purchased from the Congregational Conference. By a vote of the members, it became an interdenominational and independent congregation.

The design for most of the early churches came from the denomination of which they were member. Often the church was funded by the denomination, and they dictated what the church was going to look like.

The main entry way is in the bell tower, and the windows are colored glass.

The main building is constructed with stones from the surrounding area. The stones were hauled to the site with wagons and carefully placed in the wall with mortar.

As with most churches constructed around this time frame, the church is not adorned with a cross on the steeple. This was typical for Roman Catholic churches.

Today, most newly constructed Christian churches have crosses on the steeples.

The interior of the church is like most Christian churches; the pulpit is in the center of the chancel and the communion table is at the same level of the pews. This indicates that God came down from heaven to have communion with men.

The original pulpit is located in the fellowship hall with the open Bible printed in 1846.

For many years, it has been the custom to have an open Bible in the sanctuary. The Bible was to remain open on the pulpit from the time the church was organized until the church was disbanded. In many churches, the open Bible is now located on the communion table.

The early Bibles have some great artwork. But as time went on and more Bibles were printed, illustrations became less and less. Most of the modern Bibles are without illustrations. In the mid-1800s, when this Bible was printed, it was often used to teach the children how to read. The illustrations made this effort less difficult.

The Pulpit Bible printed in 1846.

The first illustrated printed Bible, published by Gunther Zainer of Augsburg in 1475, included woodcut initial illustrations that could be hand-colored after purchase.

For the Pilgrims, who arrived at Plymouth in 1620, the Scripture meant the Geneva Bible produced by English exiles in Calvinist Switzerland.

Chapter 15

Mary Queen of Heaven Parish, Sprague, Washington, 1882

The parish, known as Mary Queen of Heaven, is one of the oldest churches in the Spokane Catholic diocese.

Mary Queen of Heaven, Sprague Washington.

Settlers began moving to the Sprague area in the mid-1860s. One of the early settlers was Neil McGreevy. As with most settlers, as soon as they found a place to reside, their spiritual needs became a priority.

Masses for Roman Catholics was soon to follow. Father Joseph Joset, a Jesuit priest, began saying masses in 1882 in a building located just east of the present church.

The Back of the church.

In June of 1882, a committee of men decided to purchase property to construct a permanent church building. Two sites were purchased from the Northern Pacific Railroad for $50. In 1883, a wooden structure was constructed just north of the present church.

Father Aloysius Meuwese was assigned as first resident pastor by Bishop Aegidius Junger, second bishop of Nesqually, in 1885. Father Meuwese's parish encompassed an area of about 70 square miles.

The Inland Register, the official newspaper of the Diocese of Spokane, records the reaction of Father Meuwese as follows:

> *After a few minutes of friendly talk, my welcoming friends left me...And the new pastor was left alone to begin his pastoral duties. It may and does feel childish that the first thing I did was to sit down... and have a good cry. Pardon me, dear readers, but*

I was a young priest, away from all friends and relatives (the latter were in Europe), some 300 miles from a brother priest on one side and 41 miles from the Jesuit priest in Spokane Falls...However my crying spell was soon over and I entered the church and threw myself before the altar...where the picture of the Queen of Heaven cast it's glance on me.

This picture can still be seen in the choir loft of the present church loft, from where it looks down on the congregation. Finally, he returned to the rectory, and apparently being of a practical mind, found part of a broom and began sweeping out the habitation. Never again did Father Meuwese feel sad about his assignment. The first two masses were attended by 250 parishioners on the first Sunday of Advent.

The beautiful old-style brick church dominates the community of Sprague and can be seen from almost anywhere in town. The church was built under the direction of Father Van de Ven and was dedicated in October 1902. The initial cost was $7,400, with the final cost amounting to $10,000.00. The bell and the steeple came from the previous church and were incorporated in the new building.

The church design is typical European. The rounded back where the altar is located originated with the historic cathedrals. The buttresses along the sides of the building are designed to give it more lateral stability.

The round window in the front of the church designates eternity, time without end.

As with most Roman Catholic churches, the cross is visible from a great distance.

All through the ages, the cross has been a religious symbol. The Latin cross is the most common seen on churches. For many years the Roman Catholic churches were adorned with this cross. Just recently, Protestant churches began using them.

On most Northern European Protestant churches, you find the steeples with a rooster.

This is associated with the apostle Peter's denial of the Lord before the crucifixion.

In most cases, the church steeple is the tallest structure in the city or town, therefore the cross or the rooster functions as a lightning rod.

The Latin cross is the most often seen symbol representing the Christian faith.

The Celtic cross is shaped like the Latin cross, having a ring about the intersection of the shaft and crossbar.

The Greek cross has a cross that cuts through the middle by a horizontal of the same length.

Chapter 16

History "Almost" Forgotten

The first Protestant church in the East Yakima Valley was a Presbyterian church located on Mieras Road. Construction was typical of the churches built during this time period. The site was in the desert part of the state of Washington, and the closest supply of timber was the Cascade Mountains.

The local sawmill was the source of the lumber for this building. The sawmill was supplied with logs from the mountains, transported down the Yakima River during the spring runoff.

The church with the returned steeple and the old community hall.

The other building material available was stones from the local quarry several miles away. A large stained-glass window was installed in the front of the church The church bell was designed to make two different sounds for different occasions. The main clapper in the center of the bell was used to call the people to worship, while a clapper on the outside of the bell was used to notify the people in the area about special events, such as fire or war.

By 1900, most of the members moved out of the area and joined the Presbyterian church in the city of North Yakima. The church building was offered to a Dutch settlement just down the road, but after a few weeks of service this offer was declined.

The main residence of the Moxee Cattle Company was located next to the church, and the local cowboys were very disturbing to the worshippers. According to one of the local historians, on a given Sunday morning the cowboys opened the front door and rode a horse into the sanctuary during services. Since the building was no longer going to be used for worship, Mr. Antoine LaFramboise purchased the building and intended to use it as a blacksmith shop.

The Dutch settlers were planning to build their own church building 3/4 of a mile east. Mr. LaFramboise was concerned about the reaction from the community if he used the church building for a blacksmith shop, with steeple and stained-glass windows still in place, so with this in mind, he approached the Dutch settlers and made a deal. "I will let you have the steeple, the bell and the stained glass window, if you will construct a large wide door in the front wall of the building, so I can get wagons inside to work on them".

The Dutch accepted the offer. The three items were removed, and the large door was constructed as agreed upon. For 85 years, the steeple, the stained-glass window, and the bell were part of the First Reformed Church of Yakima.

In 1989, the old Reformed church building was removed to make room for a new sanctuary. Before the demolition of the old building, it was determined that the steeple should be returned to the original location.

The reformed Chruch with the borrowed steeple.

A forklift was used to transport the steeple back down the road and, with the use of a crane, was placed on the blacksmith shop.

This geographic area is known for the production of Hops. In the early days before modern machinery, the harvesting was done by hand and was very labor intensive.

At one time, workers from the Philippines were used. Some of the workers were housed in the blacksmith shop and made drawings on the wall. One of the drawings is of women with her name adjacent to the drawing.

Drawing in the south wall

The church and the adjacent outbuildings are now restored and are on the National Historic Register. The design and construction of this building are unique for this time frame. The craftsmanship is very precise and well done. The circle in front of the tower stands for eternity, time without end.

The steeple back at it's original location.

The steeple has the weathervane, typical of early Protestant churches.

This weathervane was used for target practice and, as a result it, has a few bullet holes in the ball on top.

One of the adjacent buildings is the old Community Hall, moved to this location 1/4 mile from its original location.

The stained-glass window remains in a place of honor at the east side of what is now called the East Valley Church, reflecting the sunlight during the Sunday morning worship.

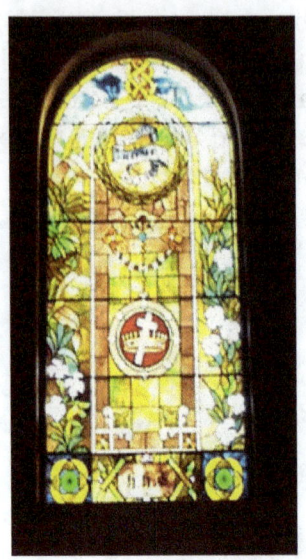

The stained glass window.

    Not much is known about the early settlers who worshipped in the church. Since the church was offered to the Dutch settlers on around 1904 not long after the settlers came to this area, it can be assumed that they did not worship in this building very long. Therefore, this chapter is called, "History 'Almost' Forgotten."

Restored Chruch building

Chapter 17
St. Michael's Episcopal Church Yakima, Washington, 1885

Information from the church archives with permission.

On September 29, 1885, during the first year of North Yakima's existence, the Rev. Dr. Rueben Nevius, a general missionary of the Pacific Northwest and a noted botanist, established the parish of St. Michael's as a mission of the diocese of Washington Territory.

St. Michaeil's Chruch, Yakima, Washington.

The church congregation was originally organized in Yakima City (now the city of Union Gap) in 1884 by Dr. Nevius and Bishop James Adams Paddock, the first Bishop of Washington.

Most of the Episcopal congregation in Yakima City participated in moving their homes and businesses to North Yakima where the Northern Pacific Railroad Company platted and promoted a new city during the extension of their line to Puget Sound. Two lots were donated to the church on the corner of Naches and Yakima Avenue. The first services were held in a small room on the second floor of a building at North Front and A Streets, and at the Moxee schoolhouse.

In 1888 Dr. Nevius formed a building committee with Colonel William Ferand Prosser, special agent of the General Land Office of Oregon and Washington and who, in 1886, was elected to Yakima County auditor; William Steinweg, who came to North Yakima in 1886 to be cashier of the First National Bank of Yakima; and Henry Blatchford Scudder and his seven children, who developed a dairy in the Moxee area.

St. Michael's Church

Plans for the new church were drawn as a gift by Edward Tuckerman Potter, a church architect from New York and Rhode Island, and were received by Mr. Scudder on June 5, 1888.

The walls of the church were built of uncut basalt stones, hauled from Garretson Grade ("Painted Rocks") by horse-drawn wagons. The stones were placed by hand in such a way to make a solid wall, joined together with mortar. The structure is Gothic in style, as noted by the shape of the windows. The three long narrow windows of cathedral glass are from Coulter and Sons of Cincinnati. The front gable of the church (west end) was carried up above the roof in three equal stages of 6 feet each and surmounted by a large stone cross. This structure seats 125 people and measures 48 feet by 25 feet with 12-foot-high walls. The main entry way is on the North side of the building, but the worshippers are facing east during the services. This follows the old European tradition, to be facing east when the Lord returns.

A large stained-glass window at the northeast corner of the sanctuary sheds light on the altar. The window is very colorful with the Archangel Michael killing the dragon.

The altar at St. Michael's

The first service at the new church was held on Christmas Day 1888, when Dr. Nevius used "God with us" as his text. The Yakima Herald newspaper reported the joyful feeling of thanksgiving. There was a good congregation present, though the number of persons connected with the mission was small.

Dr. Nevius reported that the building cost about $4,000, with $450 provided by the Women's Guild of Mission. About $600 was given by nonresident friends, including the Rev. Phillip Brooks, the writer of the Christmas hymn, "O Little Town of Bethlehem." In August 1910, the Wilson Brothers were awarded the contract for $4,564 for a hot water heating system for the building.

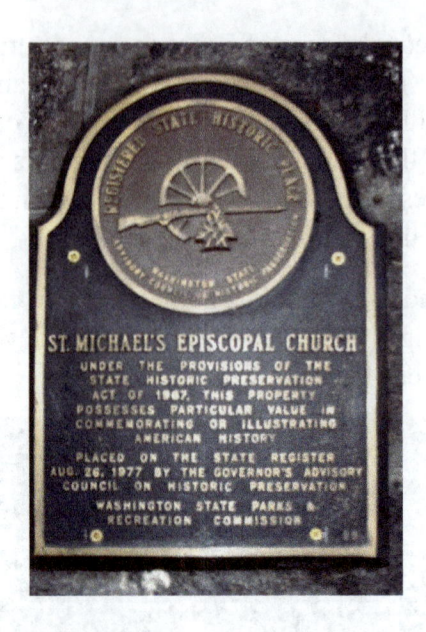

In September 1910, St. Michael's church was incorporated in the state of Washington.

The church was placed on the Washington State Historic Register on August 26, 1977.

Chapter 18

Pioneer Presbyterian Church on Clatsop Plains, Warrington, Oregon, 1850

The Pioneer Presbyterian Church on Clatsop Plains has played its part in the beginnings of Western America.

Pioneer Presbyterian Church

The Lower Columbia area has many "firsts" in its history: Robert Gray (1792) was the first over the bar of the "River of the West" and named it the "Columbia," after his American ship out of Boston. Lewis and Clark (1805-1806) were the first to cross the American continent by land and wintered at Fort Clatsop, located only a few miles from the church. John Jacob Astor (1810) sent out expeditions both by land and by the sea to establish the first American settlement on the Pacific Coast named "Astoria."

The church itself is the oldest Presbyterian Church in continuous existence west of the Rocky Mountains. The church was not the first in the territory, the Whitman Mission located near Walla Walla was established at an earlier date (1836), but it was destroyed during the Indian massacre in 1847.

William Henry Gray first came west with the Whitman party in 1836 as a lay worker. After serving with Marcus Whitman at Wailatpu and with Henry Spalding at Lapwai Mission, he migrated to the Willamette Valley and worked with Jason Lee at the Salem Mission. Around 1845, he filed a donation land claim on Clatsop Plains.

Rev. Lewis Thompson was a Presbyterian minister who graduated from Princeton Seminary in New Jersey. He was opposed to slavery and left his native Kentucky after freeing the slaves who were kept on his father's estate. He found the views supporting slavery no different in Missouri, so he joined the wagon train of 1844 to migrate to the Oregon frontier. Once here, he took up a land claim located just south of the present church property.

Rev. Thompson was invited to conduct worship services in the William Henry Gray home on September 19, 1846. By 1850, it became apparent that a permanent meeting place was both necessary and desirable. Robert Morrison gave a bond deed by which he donated one acre of land for a cemetery and four acres for a church. Morrison later received a patent to this land signed by President Grant in 1869.

The construction of the first building at this site was contracted by William H. Gray, who had been trained as a cabinet maker. The building was 20 feet by 30 feet and the total cost was $1,500. In 1873, a severe windstorm demolished this building, and the second building was constructed at the bottom of the hill just east of the present building.

This second building lasted until 1929, when the present structure was erected on the exact site of the first building. The new building was planned, but the projected cost was $15,000, well out of reach for the small congregation. The completion of the construction was assured when the daughter of Mr. and Mrs. Gray donated $10,000 for that purpose. The only condition of the gift was that the sanctuary be named the "Gray Memorial Chapel."

In 1850, a log that had washed up onto a nearby beach was hauled to the Morrison mill. From this log, Robert S. McEwan constructed a pulpit which served the church for many years.

The pulpit

When a new church was established at nearby Cannon Beach, this historic furnishing was loaned to the new congregation. From there it went to a church in Beaverton, Oregon, and after several years, it was returned to the Pioneer Presbyterian Church.

On one side, at the front of the sanctuary stands a reed organ manufactured in 1905 by the Estey Organ Company of Brattleboro, Vermont. It originally was built as a pump organ with a one-year warranty but had been made electronic prior to its coming to the Pioneer Church. It was acquired in 1949 from a church in the vicinity of Grays Harbor or Willapa Bay, Washington.

The Sanctuary with the organ and pulpit.

When the pioneers of 1845 arrived on Clatsop Plains, they had little need for a common burying ground. They were a hardy group who had survived the rigors of the long trek over the almost unmarked Oregon Trail. Robert and Nancy Morrison serve as an excellent example of these sturdy pioneers. They left Missouri on April 1, 1844, and arrived on Clatsop Plains on November 10, 1844. Nancy was later quoted as saying that she had not slept in a house during the entire journey.

The cemetery at Clatsop plains.

The need for a cemetery did arise in 1850, when a human body washed up on the beach and a young man was killed in a gunshot accident.

This prompted the Morrison family to give a plot of land for a cemetery, and the terms of their gift specified that anyone could be buried in the cemetery and that no charge for the burial was to be made.

Additional land was later purchased. Maintenance was provided by members of the community. In 1940, the cemetery was deeded to Clatsop County, who imposed a modest tax to pay for the upkeep by the county road department. One of the conditions of the change in ownership was that there would be no further burials unless the person to be buried had been a resident of the county prior to Oregon statehood in 1859.

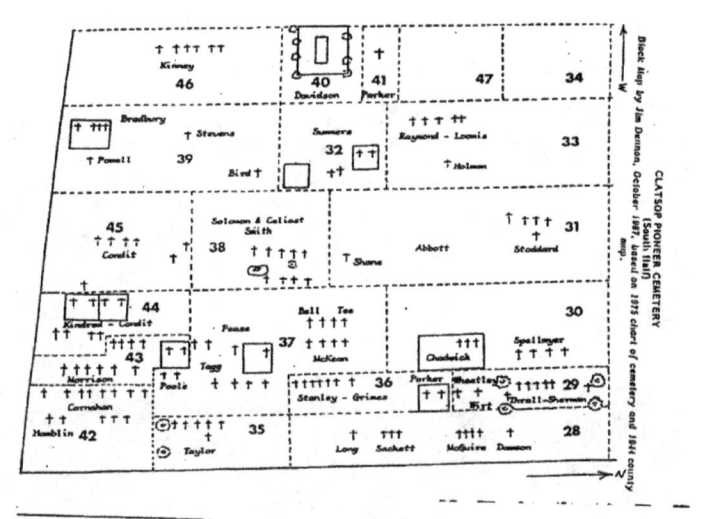

The original plot of the cemetery.

The names on the headstones in the cemetery are those of families who were genuine pioneers of this western outpost. They silently represent the kind of people who had the courage, strength, and persistence to settle this rugged Pacific Northwest coast.

One of the remaining grave markers.

For over 150 years, their faith continues to be a witness to the love of God and His Son, our Lord Jesus Christ.

Church interior.

Rev. Lewis Thompson was a Presbyterian minister who graduated from Princeton Seminary in New Jersey. He was opposed to slavery and left his native Kentucky after freeing the slaves who were kept on his father's estate. He found the views supporting slavery no different in Missouri. For this reason, he joined the wagon train of 1844 to migrate to the Oregon frontier. Once here, he took up a land claim located just south of the present church property.

Gray, who had been a Presbyterian in his home state of New York, invited Rev. Thompson to conduct services and preach a sermon in his home on September 19, 1846. Invited to join in worship were friends and neighbors, among whom were Alva and Ruth Condit, Robert and Nancy Morrison and others.

For the next four years the services alternated between the homes of the Grays and the Morrisons. By 1850 it had become apparent that a permanent meeting place was both necessary and desirable.

Chapter 19

The Church at Columbus Landing, Maryhill, Washington, 1888

This information was prepared by the Maryhill Women's Club.

In 1852, Amos Stark, the first white man to settle in Klickitat County, put ashore at Columbus Landing (now Maryhill). He was a veteran of the Mexican War and was given land for his service. After filing claim for this land at the present site of the Maryhill State Park and eastward, he left for California to search for gold.

Church at Columbus Landing.

When he returned, Mr. Stark and Wm. Hicenbotham surveyed and platted the town of Columbus, which was recorded at the courthouse in Goldendale in 1878. Amos Stark donated four lots for the church and cemetery.

Columbus had three stores, a butcher shop, a livery stable, blacksmith shop, two churches, small hospital owned by the S.P and S. Railroad, a railway depot, and hotel. The Maryhill ferry at the east end of town transported people across the Columbia River. Between 1862 and 1907, the town had about 100 residents.

It was organized as part of the Advent Christian Church. The church was built October 1888 by Amos Stark, his brother Benjamin, Wm. Chapman, Joseph Henderson, Chas. "Eddy" Bennett, John Bennett, Samuel Hope, and others.

The pews were handmade by Ben Stark, the scroll work done by Wm. Chapman, and the date above the door was lettered by W. L Sanders.

The front door of the Church

The Columbus Post Office was closed as residents began moving away, and the church fell into disrepair. During the 1970s, the community banded together to restore the building. The pews were recovered from storage in a barn. The ceiling, floor, and windows were replaced. The glass above the door was restored by a grandson of W.L. Sanders. The hanging lights are from a 100-year-old home.

The Advent Christian Denomination formed their association in 1860. They were followers of the teachings of William Miller, a farmer of New York State. He began an intensive study of the Bible around 1818. He compared scripture to scripture and was convinced that the second coming of Christ would occur about 1843. He began to speak in 1831, when invited, that the second coming would be soon. People of many denominations, plus unbelievers, soon followed him. They were called Millerites. Miller stressed inter-denominational meetings, and as many as five publications surfaced during his public preaching years.

The date of Christ's return was set for October 22, 1844, and when this did not occur it was labeled "The Great Disappointment."

Although Miller was against forming a new denomination, history records that five different denominations came from the Millerite movement. Dr William Chapman, M.D., an active Advent Christian preacher in Iowa, left for the Washington Territory in 1878. He was instrumental in organizing and building the Maryhill Church.

In 1969, the Advent Christian Willamette Valley Conference donated the church building to the Maryhill Women's Club. As of 1994, there were 340 Advent Christian Churches in North America, with 22 in the Western states.

In 1991, the Maryhill church was granted historic status from the Washington State Preservation Office and the national office.

Chapter 20

First Presbyterian Church, Bickleton, Washington, 1903

The city of Bickleton is in Klickitat County in the state of Washington.

This community is known as the "Bluebird Capital of America" because thousands of bluebirds spend most of the year in the area. More than 1500 bird houses have been erected by the residents. There are two kinds of bluebirds here: the all-blue Mountain

Bluebird and the red-breasted Western Bluebird. Although the town is small (population 90 in 2003), there are interesting events and places in the area. Bickleton is home to the state's oldest tavern and rodeo.

This community is in the center of a large dry land wheat farming region.

Birdhouse in front of church.

The Presbyterian church is the center of spiritual and social activity for the people in this region.

Excerpts from the centennial publication: "Footprints through the Years".

In the sanctuary of the Bickleton Presbyterian Church, it is written on one of the stained-glass windows that the First Presbyterian Church was founded in 1903 by Lysander Coleman, and so it was. But its roots go back to the first sermon preached in the Bickleton area in 1876 by Methodist minister, Rev J. H. Allyn at the R.M. Graham ranch on Alder Creek.

In the fall of 1880, Mr. Allyn became the first pastor of the Methodist society organized that year in Bickleton. The record shows that the first church service held was the quarterly meeting on September 19, 1880, in a schoolhouse.

Our roots grew still more from the influence of the Cleveland Presbyterian church organized in 1884, through the efforts of Rev.

L.J. Thompson.

A number of German families settled a few miles north and east of Bickleton. One of the first things they did was build a church. The Bickleton News for January 1, 1904, stated that a Christmas program was held in the German Lutheran church east of Bickleton and was well-attended. The children did their part to satisfy every Christmas-loving person present.

Stained glass window with the words: "L. Coleman founder 1903."

A Danish Lutheran church also provided roots that have fed our church. The Rev. Plambeck preached in the Danish language in the German Lutheran Church, as they had no building of their own. A pastor by the name of Jens Jessen came and made his home with Mr. and Mrs. Steve Matsen. They met in the homes of members once a month. The first confirmation class under the tutelage of Pastor Jessen was held in June of 1909 in the German Lutheran Church.

The mothers and daughters came by team with cream cans full of water and cleaned the church so it would be presentable for the day when the young people would be giving their hearts to Christ. They also filled the church with lilacs, and the smell was so strong that Alfred Jensen fainted during the ceremony.

The history of the Presbyterian Church began on April 18, 1903, when a meeting was called at the Clanton-Mitty and Co. Hall, for the purpose of organizing a Presbyterian church in Bickleton. All who were interested in church work were invited. The Rev. James Thompson of north Yakima was the moderator at this meeting. Permission was received from the Methodists to have services in their church, providing it did not interfere with their services.

Definite plans were made to erect a church building in 1903. Mrs. McCredy, accompanied by her son Clarence, canvassed the country soliciting funds for a building.

They first went through the Dot area with a horse and a cart, but Mr. McCredy thought this was too hard for his wife, so he bought a covered wagon for her to use to finish the job. When she had raised $1,200 in cash and subscriptions, the work on the building began.

By spring of 1904, the Presbyterian Society had become an incorporate church. The church had a membership of 33.

Bell tower with bell.

A few years later the young men of the community decided to purchase a bell for the church. Mr. V.W. Harshberger, a Bickleton grocer, bought the bell in Portland and brought it to Bickleton. It was installed and dedicated in May 1908, and it is still in use today.

All during the next one hundred years, the church saw many changes.

The most difficult times came when it was very hard to keep a pastor for a long period of time. On several occasions, the pastor was shared with other congregations.

In the Sanctuary

The sanctuary shows the close relationship the church has with the American Natives from the area.

Chapter 21

Tualatin Plains Presbyterian Church, Old Scotch Church, 1873

Information from the History of the Tualatin Plains Presbyterian church.

The organization of the Tualatin Plains Presbyterian Church is recorded on the first page of the minutes of the Session, in the time-faded hand of its first pastor, the Rev. George Ross.

The Old Scotch Church

The words of this venerable saga were set down in the following manner:

> *Columbia academy, Washington County, Oregon, 16th November 1873. After a sermon this day by Rev. A.L. Lindsley, D.D., Portland, Oregon, he along with two of his elders, Messrs. Holman and Wadhams, organized the Tualatin Plains Presbyterian Church, consisting of twelve members. The sacrament of the Lord's supper was dispensed. The congregation then proceeded to select two elders, when Messrs. William Chalmers and James Smith were chosen to fill that office. It was found that Mr. Chalmers was an ordained elder, he having been chosen and set apart to that office a long time previous to his departure from Scotland. He was received and Mr. smith ordained to the eldership of the Tualatin Plains Church. Closed with prayer.*

The charter members came mostly from the same area in Aberdeenshire, west of Aberdeen, Scotland. They were previously members of the "Free Church of Scotland." Upon coming to Oregon, all settled in the same area on the Tualatin Plains.

From their Scottish origin, this church acquired the name it is more often identified with today, "The Old Scotch Church." Most of the twelve Scottish pioneers remained in the area and in the church all their lives. Eight of the twelve, and many of their descendants, are presently at rest in the cemetery surrounding the church.

Church cemetery

Upon organization, the congregation began examining the countryside for a site on which to build a new church and cemetery. Regarding this quest, the following passage is found in the session minutes:

> *At a congregational meeting held at the home of William Chalmers, Rev. George Ross, acting as chairman, it was unanimously agreed to buy two acres of land from Jacob Hoover as a site for a church and burying ground. Mr. Hoover, being present, very generously said, "I will donate one acre to you and sell you the other for $25.00." The offer was accepted and the thanks at the meeting given to Mr. Hoover for his liberality.*

The site they chose was beautifully set among firs, near the bank of McKay creek about four miles north of Hillsboro.

The words of this venerable saga were set down in the following manner:

> **Columbia academy, Washington County, Oregon, 16th November 1873. After a sermon this day by Rev. A.L. Lindsley, D.D., Portland, Oregon, he along with two of his elders, Messrs. Holman and Wadhams, organized the Tualatin Plains Presbyterian Church, consisting of twelve members. The sacrament of the Lord's supper was dispensed. The congregation then proceeded to select two elders, when Messrs. William Chalmers and James Smith were chosen to fill that office. It was found that Mr. Chalmers was an ordained elder, he having been chosen and set apart to that office a long time previous to his departure from Scotland. He was received and Mr. smith ordained to the eldership of the Tualatin Plains Church. Closed with prayer.**

The charter members came mostly from the same area in Aberdeenshire, west of Aberdeen, Scotland. They were previously members of the "Free Church of Scotland." Upon coming to Oregon, all settled in the same area on the Tualatin Plains.

From their Scottish origin, this church acquired the name it is more often identified with today, "The Old Scotch Church." Most of the twelve Scottish pioneers remained in the area and in the church all their lives. Eight of the twelve, and many of their descendants, are presently at rest in the cemetery surrounding the church.

Church cemetery

Upon organization, the congregation began examining the countryside for a site on which to build a new church and cemetery. Regarding this quest, the following passage is found in the session minutes:

> *At a congregational meeting held at the home of William Chalmers, Rev. George Ross, acting as chairman, it was unanimously agreed to buy two acres of land from Jacob Hoover as a site for a church and burying ground. Mr. Hoover, being present, very generously said, "I will donate one acre to you and sell you the other for $25.00." The offer was accepted and the thanks at the meeting given to Mr. Hoover for his liberality.*

The site they chose was beautifully set among firs, near the bank of McKay creek about four miles north of Hillsboro.

The Church and cemetery

 Now that a site had been chosen and the land acquired, plans went ahead for construction. At a congregational meeting on March 11, 1878, the board of trustees was requested to acquire plans and specifications for a church building and the *probable* cost, then report their findings at the next meeting. At the following congregational meeting, a simple Gothic design proposed by Mr. Balantyne with a probable cost of $2,120 was accepted.

 The plan called for a tall eight-sided steeple, buttresses on the outer walls, a steep roof, and stained-glass windows. This style was probably selected because of its similarity to their home church in Scotland.

 Construction began immediately with much of the labor donated by church members and men and women of the community. The lumber of the building came from nearby forests, processed by mills in the vicinity. With donated labor and materials, the building was rapidly completed and dedicated in 1878.

 Along with the construction of the church building, work also progressed on the cemetery plot. The land was cleared and readied for burial purposes. The first person laid to rest in this peaceful cemetery was Margaret Smith Chalmers, the daughter of William and Catherine Chalmers, who died May 28, 1876 at the age of six years and nine months. Inscribed on the gravestone were the child's last words: "The lamb has come for me, He's come."

The original sanctuary furnishings were donated by members and friends of the congregation, including the pulpit, large pulpit Bible, sterling communion service, and the communion table. All of these are still in use today. The pews came from the Methodist Church in old Glencoe (now North Plains).

In 1986, a beautiful handcrafted Celtic cross was hung in the chancel. It was made from a dogwood tree that had grown for many years in the cemetery.

Church interior and the Celtic cross.

(1910 BULLETIN)

Sunday, May 8th 1910

10:15 Sunday School
11:00 Bible Training
    Birthday Offering
11:15 Worship
    Hymn 291
    Talk to Chik'ren
    Childrens' Hymn 305 (Seated)
    Scripture lesson
    Prayer
    Offertory
    Sermon, Ministry of the Spirit
    Hymn 187
    Benediction (Seated)
    Silent Prayer
2:30 Sunday School at Glencoe
7:00 C. E. Subject, Christian Graces
8:00 Sermon, The New Birth

Announcements

Mr. J. A. Paterson of Portland will speak next Sunday on his experiences in Africa while establishing the Livingstone Mission.

The pastor expects this church, with all its societies to give, for Missions at Home $200., for Missions Abroad $100. Last year the amounts were $187.85 and $51 respectively.

The publisher of the Calander expresses his appreciation for the generous response of last Sunday.

The Sunday School Council considered two important matters last Sunday: 1st, the adopting of a cradle roll if somebody could be found to superintend it, and 2nd, the securing of temperance pledges from every member of the Sunday School.

Oregon Going Dry!

The Memory Hymn for this month was written by a Catholic Monk, Bernard of Clairvaux, about the year 1150 A. D.

The C. E. Meeting at Glencoe last Sunday night was well attended. The service had an attendance of 43.

Christ saves "unto the uttermost." In return He wants us to do our utmost to evangelize the world in our generation.

Church bulletin from 1910.

Chapter 22

St Paul's Lutheran Church, Douglas, Washington, 1889

St. Paul's Lutheran Church

It was on September 23, 1889, when a group of men, mostly German immigrants, met to discuss the need for a place to worship. As an immigrant myself, I know the need of gathering with people from your country of origin. The time and effort they put into constructing this church tells us the deep-rooted faith the immigrants possessed.

From the cornerstone to the location of the pulpit, the construction of the building has the European flavor.

The cornerstone has the German word "Kirch" for church and the date.

Cornerstone laying is only performed on school buildings, public structures, or places of worship. The cornerstone may be of any dimension—granite, marble, brass or other compounds. Often, a cavity is cut on the backside of the stone to contain information regarding this event.

The corner stone at St. Paul's.

The preacher entered the pulpit through a special door from the meeting room. The pulpit was located on the left side of the altar, and half-way up the front wall. The pulpit in the early churches was elevated so everyone could see the person giving the sermon. We must keep in mind that in the early days, the ladies were all wearing hats, and sometimes they were large hats. If the sermon was given from the same level as the altar, not many people could see him.

The altar is well preserved and in good condition. It has a very nice painting of a shepherd holding a lamb. An inscription at the bottom of the altar is written in German, **"Der Herr ist mein Hirte,"** or "The Lord is my Shepherd."

The white and gold are symbolic of heaven.

The altar

The book of Revelations mentions the great white throne, and gold is mentioned several times.

At one time the city of Douglas had a population of about 200; now it is approximately 40. The general store is the hub of the community, and a good attempt is being made to bring back the history of the area.

The church is now on the Historic Register, and the present owner is committed to restore the church to what it was when it was first constructed.

Just recently, a pump organ was donated as a valuable item to the restoration effort.

The pump organ

Most of the churches built at the turn of the century and still in use have the bathroom facilities inside.

At St Paul's church, the original bathroom facilities, the "Outhouse," is still standing behind the building.

The outhouse

As the sun set behind the steeple, we were reminded of God's faithfulness to us. The cross could be seen from a great distance, and we were reminded about men's faith in God, a God who was willing to send His son to die for mankind.

The early immigrants demonstrated their love for God in building a house of worship.

It is up to our generation to preserve that heritage for the next generation.

The following information was received from the Douglas Community Historical Association.

Interior of St. Paul's Lutheran Church 1960

    The years from 1880 until 1890 brought the big wave of homesteaders to Douglas County, Washington. The early explorers of the Pacific Northwest were in the past, the fur traders, miners, and prospectors were becoming extinct, and the day of the big cattlemen was being superseded by the homesteader with his wagon and plow. One of the first men to plow the virgin soil in Douglas County was Ole Ruud, who arrived May 8, 1883.

    Immigrant trains were boarded in Illinois or other eastern points. At Ritzville, the end of the rail line, many eager men blazed a path alone or with families, outfitted themselves with a wagon and a plow, and chose Douglas County as their new home.

Jacob Bunger was one of the first German immigrants, and it is said that he was instrumental to attracting more of his fellow countrymen to the area.

They found pioneer life in this new country beset with difficulties. The winter of 1888-1889 was a notorious one because of its length and severity. The previous winter had been mild and consequently, the settlers were not prepared for the "hard winter." Stories are legion of hardships and tragedies experienced.

Chapter 23

St. James Episcopal Church, Cashmere, Washington

Information from Steeples and Peoples By A.J. Kjack

St. James Episcopal Church.

    The first settlers in this area were Catholic priests who established a mission in 1863. Others came here and settled as farmers. The town was called the Old Mission, and sometimes referred to just as Mission.

    Soon the farmers found out that this area was arid and desert-like and not much would grow without water. In many cases, small rock dams were placed in the river to divert water into irrigation ditches. The first apples were shipped out in the fall of 1903.

In 1904, the town wanted to incorporate, but the name had to be changed since there already was a town with the name Mission in the state of Washington.

Judge James A. Chase had traveled to India and decided that the area resembled the land around the Vale of Kasmir. This is how the name of Cashmere came about.

In 1890, Mrs. Sherman, who arrived in Colorado from England in 1885, came here by wagon. She missed her church so much that she was determined to get a church started here.

A building site was purchased on Division Street, and a wooden structure was built. The site and the building were not satisfactory, and a new location was found.

Mrs. Sherman wanted a stone church at a different location. This resulted in a donated site by Mr. and Mrs. Sherman, and since Mr. Sherman was a stone mason, a stone church was constructed on Cottage Avenue.

Stone wall at St. James church

Wood was the most often-used building material during this time period. It was readily available and not difficult to use.

Stone could be found at several locations as construction

material. This material was more difficult to construct but much longer-lasting than wood. Stone construction was also easier to maintain.

It was a few more years before brick came to be used as building material in the Northwest for smaller buildings such as churches.

The early brickyards were sometimes called wheelbarrow yards, meaning that most of the material needed to make bricks could be loaded on a wheelbarrow and hauled to the location where bricks were needed. This was provided that the material available was suitable to make bricks. Transportation, because of the weight of the bricks and the lack of good roads, made it more feasible to move the yard than haul the bricks.

When the church was completed, Mrs. Sherman was given the opportunity to name the church. She gave the church the same name that was given to the church she attended in England, St. James.

During World War I, church service was sporadic, and no church school was held.

Front door of the church

In the 1930s, the Rev. Oliver Cleveland became the pastor and remained the leader for 20 years.

Rev. Cleveland made the lantern shades from banana crates and stained glass he salvaged. He led the church through the difficult years of the Great Depression.

Chapter 24

Holy Trinity Temple Russian Orthodox Church, Wilkeson, Washington, 1896

This parish was founded in the eastern Pierce County town of Wilkeson in the state of Washington in 1896.

Church with blue "onion dome" cupola

It was founded under the auspices of the Russian Orthodox Church. In 1970, the Russian Orthodox Church granted the North American Church administrative independence, forming the Orthodox Church in America.

The city of Wilkeson is known for a rich history in coal mining. Coal was mined for the Great Northern Railroad and the city of Tacoma.

In the late 1700s, Russian missionaries traveled by ship and then by kayak to bring Orthodox Christianity to the Aleuts and Eskimos throughout Alaska. From there, they came to the Northwest to follow the mining trade. As with most immigrants to this country, an attempt was made to maintain the "Old Country" atmosphere as much as possible.

Priority number one for those immigrants was the Russian Orthodox Church.

A typical mining cart on display at Wilkeson

As these settlers began their life in Wilkeson, another coal mining town was being established in eastern Washington known as Cle Elum.

The major reason Orthodox Christianity is so little known in most of the United States is that most of the people who originally settled in America came from western Europe, not from Greece,

Russia, or the Middle East. For the first thousand years of church history, the church was essentially one.

The five historic patriarchal centers were Jerusalem, Antioch, Rome, Alexandria, and Constantinople. There were occasional heretical schismatic groups going their own way, but to be sure, but the church was unified until the 11th century.

Then, in events culminating in A.D. 1054, the Roman Patriarch pulled away from the other four, pursuing his long-developing claim of universal headship of the church. Today, nearly a thousand years later, the other four Patriarchates remain intact, in full communion, maintaining that Orthodox Apostolic Faith.

Many significant differences began to develop: differences in worship, theology, and church government. The result of this gradual pulling apart was that, over a period of centuries–from the ninth to the thirteenth–the churches of the West and the churches of the East officially broke communication with each other.

A timeline of Church history by Fr. Marc Dunaway in "What is the Orthodox church?"

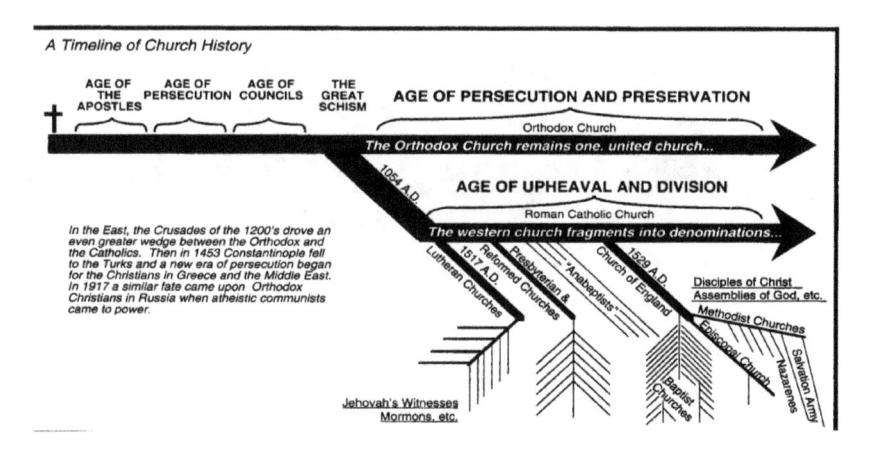

A Timeline of Church History

AGE OF THE APOSTLES | AGE OF PERSECUTION | AGE OF COUNCILS | THE GREAT SCHISM | AGE OF PERSECUTION AND PRESERVATION

Orthodox Church

The Orthodox Church remains one, united church...

1054 A.D.

AGE OF UPHEAVAL AND DIVISION

Roman Catholic Church

The western church fragments into denominations...

In the East, the Crusades of the 1200's drove an even greater wedge between the Orthodox and the Catholics. Then in 1453 Constantinople fell to the Turks and a new era of persecution began for the Christians in Greece and the Middle East. In 1917 a similar fate came upon Orthodox Christians in Russia when atheistic communists came to power.

Lutheran Churches, Reformed Churches, Presbyterian, Anabaptists, Church of England, 1517 A.D., 1529 A.D., Jehovah's Witnesses, Mormons, etc., Baptist Churches, Disciples of Christ, Assemblies of God, etc., Methodist Churches, Episcopal Church, Salvation Army, Nazarenes

In the Orthodox tradition, the faithful stand through nearly the entire service. In some churches, you will not find the familiar church pew. A few chairs will be located along the wall for the members who cannot stand through the entire service.

The pungent odor of incense is heavy during the service. Music will take up about seventy-five percent during the service without instruments. A small choir will lead the congregation in a *cappella* harmony.

The onion dome is a feature that frequently adorns the Orthodox Churches, and the domes are often brightly painted. The colors represent different aspects of religion. Green, blue, and gold domes represent the Holy Trinity. Black domes represent submission. Blue domes represent heaven. Onion domes often appear in groups of three or five, representing the Holy Trinity or Jesus and the four Evangelists.

The blue onion dome.

John & Esther VanBelle

Chapter 25

Visitation Catholic Church, Verboort Oregon, 1875

Excerpts from church records.

In the month of February 1875, six Hollandish or Dutch families arrived at Portland, Oregon, with the intention to start a Catholic colony in that state. They hailed from De Pere, Brown County, Wisconsin's Diocese of Green Bay, where their nation and creed were represented in great numbers.

The aged John Verboort (senior), his wife Theodora de Rayt, and their eldest son John Verboort (junior) were among them. After having looked around in different localities, they resolved to buy the Black place in Washington County, about four miles northwest of Cornelius.

The history of the Catholic community of Verboort, Oregon is at least indirectly related to the conditions of nineteenth century Europe. The famine of 1846 hit most of Europe, and the depression that followed.

Extreme poverty existed, and children at the age of 10 years were entered into the workforce. In the spring of 1848, Mr. and Mrs. John Verboort and their four children left Holland for a 58-day voyage to America. They landed in Boston on May 5, 1848. From there, they traveled by flatboat and wagon to De Pere, Wisconsin.

In 1875, after long winters and many hardships, they left Wisconsin and came to Oregon. They traveled by train to San Francisco by ship to Astoria, Oregon and by boat to Portland.

As with most immigrants, as soon as a place was found to settle, a need arose to have a place to worship.

This church was constructed in 1941.
The existing structure was destroyed by fire.

Rev. Augustine Verboort was transferred from the diocese of Milwaukee to the new settlement. He bought an organ and a bell, and had it shipped, but the bell did not arrive until after his death.

Soon after Father Verboort arrived, the people began to construct a temporary chapel of rough lumber. It was blessed September 19, 1875.

In the beginning of June 1883, the construction of a new church was started.

This church was destroyed by fire in 1941.

The Verboort community is one of the very few that was able to maintain their European roots. The majority of the names on the church roster originated in Holland. Another Dutch community is located in Lynden, Washington. Those settlers were all Protestant while the settlers at Verboort were Roman Catholic.

Both communities are dedicated to their churches and their belief systems.

The division that exists between the two denominations in Holland was brought to America and remains to this day.

The parish grounds have stately Sequoia Redwood trees donated by John Ramsey Porter, probably in the fall of 1883.

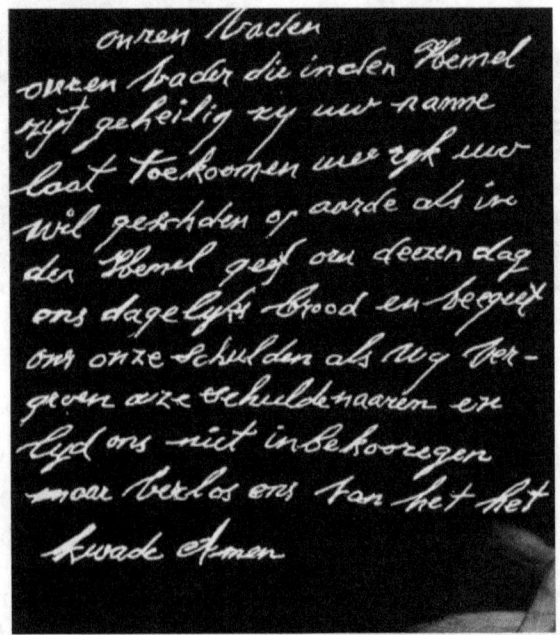

The Lord's Prayer in the Holland language.

John & Esther VanBelle

The Redwood Trees

Verboort
VISITATION CATHOLIC CHURCH
4265 NW Visitation Road
Forest Grove, Oregon 97116

June 26, 2000

Dear Parishioners and Friends in Christ,

Early parishioners at Verboort expected the parish to be here a long time, so they planted redwood trees which take a long time to grow.

The giant sequoia redwood trees on the parish grounds are a landmark in the area, and are witness to a parish and its people noted for their deep spirituality and loyalty to the faith.

It is with joy that we mark 125 years of Visitation Parish. We are honored and deeply grateful. God will continue to bless our parish.

Sincerely,

Rev. Joseph Heuberger
Pastor

Chapter 26

St. Joseph's Catholic Church, Waterville, Washington, 1892

St. Joseph's Catholic Church

Source: Steeples and Peoples by A.J.Kjac

Waterville is the highest incorporated community, elevation wise, in the State of Washington at 2,650 feet. Waterville lies in a valley just north of Badger Mountain. The downtown district is listed on the national Register of Historic Places. Waterville is also the county seat for Douglas County.

The St. Joseph's parish was founded in 1892 with a small

church being built under the direction of Father DeRouge. By 1915, however, the congregation had outgrown this little church and the present brick building was constructed.

The church is a landmark to travelers along Highway 2 as you enter the town of Waterville from the east.

Father O'Connor served from 1923-1927, during which time crop failures were common and services were held in the basement conserve on the heat bill.

*Typical eastern Washington home.
Located at the Pioneer Park in Union Gap Washington*

In 1937, the first church bell was installed, and a new roof put on. Under the leadership of Father Paul Flad, a pipe organ was installed in the church in 1959.

The church is a beautiful brick building. When compared with the homes that were constructed about the same time frame, it is evident the importance of the church to the community.

The workmanship is exceptional for a building constructed at this location.

The first brickyard was started in Waterville in 1889 to replace the wood structures, which were considered temporary and a fire hazard.

The round rose window in the front of the building is typical of most churches representing eternity, without end.

Chapter 27
St. Peter's, The Dalles Oregon, 1848

Information from the Old St. Peter's Landmark Preservation, Inc.

The town began as an Indian home many years before white men came. The Indians called the area "*Win-Quatt,*" meaning "a place encircled by rocks." Lewis and Clark were the first white men in the area and camped here in October of 1805.

Help came to the immigrants traveling the Oregon Trail. The Dalles was named by French-Canadian trappers. The meaning of the word is close to "a place where water is confined by rocks."

The year 1838 was to see new arrivals in the Dalles, Oregon Country. The Rev. Lee, Rev. Jason Lee's nephew, and his associate H.K. Perkins, were appointed to serve here.

The church as it now exists.

On May 16, 1848, the Rev. Rousseau was appointed to the first Catholic Church at the Dalles.

The first church was a log cabin erected in 1848. The church building had mats on the walls and floor. This church burned on February 26 when the matting caught fire from a candle. The early records were lost in this fire.

The second building was made of sawed lumber and had a steeple.

The first entry in the records notes that 417 adults and children attended.

Of these, 117 were white and 300 were Indian. As the Parish grew, a third building was constructed "downtown" in 1862. This building was replaced with a brick structure that has now become a national landmark.

St. Peter's Landmark was built in 1898. The landmark has been used as a benchmark for laying out property lines. This was a common practice before official surveys were available. In 1890, a committee was formed consisting of Max Vogt, Henry Herbring, E.P Fitzgerald, and Jacob Fritz to begin planning a new brick church to replace the old wooden structure. Plans were obtained by Herbring from architect Rinklage of Munster of Westphalia, Germany. Otto Kleeman, a Portland architect, drew details and specifications.

Construction was delayed until May 1, 1897, by events such as a huge fire that burned much of the town, depression, crop failure, and low prices.

On July 25, 1897, the cornerstone was laid. The steeple rises 176 feet in the air, topped by a 6-foot weathervane in the form of a rooster. The rooster was manufactured by Frank S. Gunning. The weathervane turns on bearings, which have never needed replacement or repairs. The rooster symbolizes the denial of Jesus by Peter. Jesus foretold Peter's denial before the cock would crow. The crow is also known as the bird of light since ancient times.

The steeple and weathervane.

The roof was galvanized iron Spanish tile and was replaced in 1995 with tile designed in Canada to match the original.

At the four corners of the steeple are special downspouts called gargoyles; they are shaped like a lion's heads and the purpose is to keep water from the foundation.

A statue of St. Peter is looking down at the people entering the main entrance to the church.

Statue of St. Peter

In the vestibule is the belfry rope, connected to a 533-pound bell. On special occasions the bell rope is pulled, and the glorious sounds ring out across the town.

The church interior has six rose windows. Rose windows are very common in many churches, they are round and represent eternity, a circle without end.

The Povey Stained Glass window.

There are 34 stained glass windows made by the famous Povey brothers of Portland Oregon. The cherubs were designed to portray the daughters of one of the Povey brothers. Most of the windows were donated in memory of pioneer families.

Music has been a very important part of the worship experience since ancient history. It was Miriam, the sister of Moses, who led the women in a song of victory and gratitude. King David is well known for his psalms and the use of musical instruments.

St. Peter's has a Kilgen pipe organ made of rare tiger wood, which was installed in 1927. Research reveals that the Kilgen Pipe Organ Company was established in 1851 and one of the top ten organ makers in the United States.

A collapsible pump organ circa 1880 is located next to the altar. This organ was used by Fr. Bronsgeest as he traveled from parish to parish, including the Dalles and outlying areas. This type of organ has been in use by the United States Army chaplains as a field organ for many years. The air to operate this organ is provided by two-foot paddles. The organ player could control the volume by using the lever at the front of the organ.

The serene, lovely Madonna, carved from the keel of a ship sunk off the San Francisco coast in the early 1850s, was a gift from the Vogts & Chapmans in memory of a relative saved from the shipwreck. The statue is well preserved and carved in minute details.

Madonna and the Tabernacle

The compartment below the statue is called the tabernacle, in it are the elements of the Eucharist.

The railings and altars were made in Italy from Carrara marble and installed by artisans from Italy.

John & Esther VanBelle

The Altar

The Baptismal

Chapter 28

Coupeville United Methodist Church, Coupeville Washington

Information from the Coupeville Examiner dated Friday April 4, 2003, with permission.

Coupeville United Methodist Church

"We only number six families and about fifteen children at present, most of them are too small to go to school. There are eighteen bachelors and youth residing on the island, but we want more families, so we can have schools and churches for ourselves and our children."

-Rebecca Ebey, February 21, 1853.

American settlers on Whidbey Island hungered for the closeness of a religious congregation. The Oregon Conference of the Methodist Episcopal Church answered that call 150 years ago, in April 1853. They sent the Reverends Benjamin Close and young W.B. Morse to explore religious fervor in the villages of Puget Sound.

The itinerant preachers recalled their journey to Whidbey Island from Vancouver, Washington Territory:

> *We purchased a canoe in partnership and came as far as Olympia in that... From Olympia we came on foot some 60 miles to the Cowlitz landing, carrying our saddle bags; made this distance in two days.*
>
> *We might have had a horse for $10, but we thought walking nearly as easy as riding on horseback [as there were no roads in 1853].*

Selecting a community in which to build a church in the wilderness demanded careful consideration of spiritual needs balanced by economics. Itinerant preachers of the Methodist church were granted only meager stipends—about $50 to $100 annually. There were no church buildings on Whidbey Island in 1853; there was not a school or public building for meetings.

Families hosted Reverend Morse in their homes, providing food, shelter, and a place for worship. The first American wedding and the first funeral on Whidbey Island were solemnized by Benjamin Close.

Coupeville residents maintained friendly relations with local Indians but, fearing marauding northern tribes, built or converted cabins into blockhouses for communal security.

Between 1855 and 1856, some families lived in blockhouses for months at a time.

The church interior.

Calista Kinney Lovejoy, whose seafaring husband was gone many months of the year, took shelter with her children in the Alexander blockhouse, now on exhibit in Coupeville.

One of the first children, Howard Bartlett Lovejoy, would become the designer and builder of historic Coupeville Methodist Church which is preserved and in use today.

One description survives in its archives: "The church was not a large building; there was a row of seats on either side and an aisle down the middle with a space at the end of the aisle for the pulpit which was a small stand. The ladies sat on one side of the aisle and the gents on the other."

The white population in 1853, north of the Colubia River to the 49th Parallel, barely exceeded 3,000 people. Due to the sparse population, women held elected and appointed government position. Between 1884 and 1888, they voted in local and federal elections. When church members demanded that pastors should be married so that their wives could teach Sunday school, play the piano for services, clean the church, and welcome bachelors at the parsonage, Coupeville women stepped forward to suspend these heartless demands.

The construction of new roads and homes in the heart of town displaced the 1859 church structure in the midst of the prairie on Grove Terry's former property. In the early 1870s, the Coupe family donated an acre of land for the church. Times were rough. Captain Coupe died in 1873, but in 1857 the dwindling Methodist membership managed to move the frame structure to its Prairie Center location.

Typical northwest homestead. Located at the museum at The Dallas Oregon.

A visitor to the island remarked in 1880, "Much of this portion if the island is the richest kind of prairie land and is now owned by old sea captains who don't know any too much about farming. The people are generally well- to-do, many of them are forehanded and are said to be generous; though there seems to be a cloud on the religious position of the island."

Chapter 29

Saint Joseph's Mission, Nez Perce Indian Reservation, 1874 (Also called Slickpoo Mission)

St. Joesph's Mission

    The Saint Joseph's Mission, also known as the Silkpoo Mission, is located east of Lewiston, Idaho. It is a semi-active Roman Catholic church that was built in 1874 in the former community of Slickpoo, Idaho.

Father J.M. Cataldo developed the Jesuit Nez Perce Mission that continued long after he founded Gonzaga University in Spokane, Washington. He was very successful working with the Indians of several northwest tribes.

The Nez Perce Indians lived in Idaho, Washington, and Oregon, west of the Rocky Mountains.

They called themselves the Nimiipu (NEE-me-poo) tribe, which meant "the real people." The French explorers gave them the name of "*Nez-perce*," the French word for "pierced noses." The people they saw with pierced noses were from a different tribe, they were mistaken, but the name did stick until this day. Men women and children all had their different jobs. The men did the hunting and fishing. The women took care of the washing, basket making, and the everyday chores. The children practiced skills they would need when they became adults. The boys would practice horseback riding and archery. The girls practiced weaving and corn grinding. This process took several years, before they would be allowed to perform the duties of the adults.

The Nez Perce tribe had different types of guardian spirits

called weyekin (WEE-ya-kins), which would protect them from harm. To receive weyekin, the young girl or boy around the age of 12 to 15 would go to the mountain to fast. There, he or she would receive a vision of a spirit that would take the form of a mammal or a bird. There was also a creator, Hanyawat (han-ya-WAT), the Great Spirit or maker of all things.

Chief Joseph, known by his people as In-mut-too-ya-lat-lat ("thunder coming up over the land from the water"), was best known for his resistance to the U.S government's attempt to force his tribe onto reservations. Joseph spent much of his childhood at a mission maintained by Christian missionaries.

Chief Joseph was a man with great insights and many of his quotes are recorded. One quote reflects his early upbringing at the mission.

> **We were thought to believe that the Great Spirit sees and hears everything, and never forgets, that hereafter he will give every man a spirit home according to his deserts: If he has been a good man, he will have a good home, if he has been a bad man, he will have a bad home.**

Chief Joseph died in 1905 at the age of 60, alone and forgotten by most. He was buried on the Colville Reservation away from the home of his ancestors. In 1928, his descendants decided to move his body to the shores of Wallowa Lake. It was discovered that Chief Joseph's skull had been removed.

This confirmed the rumor that it had been on display somewhere. May God forgive the perpetrators of this terrible act.

John & Esther VanBelle

Chapter 30

Saint Mary's Church, White Swan, Washington, 1887

St. Mary's Catholic Church

    A meeting of Yakama Indians with the Rev. Victor Garrand, S.J. in 1887 resulted in plans for a Roman Catholic Church in White Swan, located on the Yakama Indian Reservation.

In most parts of the world, Europeans first brought the Gospel to the natives. But in the Northwest, other Indians had a great influence in bringing the Gospel. The first Native American "missionaries" were Iroquois, from the East Coast. The area between Montana and Eastern Washington was the Land of the Flatheads, a people with many gods. Before the Black Robes arrived, there were exotic stories about the Christian God.

They were the people who brought the stories about the white men in black robes, who could lead people to the Happy Hunting Grounds. In 1816, a group of 24 Iroquois from the Great Lakes came to live among the Flatheads and shared their stories. From there it spread to the other tribes and bands in the Northwest.

In July of 1889, Charlie Mann offered four acres for the new mission and cemetery located along Toppenish Creek, 300 yards southeast of the present church.

First White Swan Church 1889.

This generous offer was accepted by Bishop Aegidius Junger, bishop of Nesqually.

In August 1889, Indian carpenter Joseph Yahotalwit became

the foreman of the construction project. Pine logs were brought by team to the Indian Mill Creek sawmill.

Mother Katharin Drexel was declared blessed by Pope John. Paul VI supplied the nails, paint, doors, and windows.

Interior of the church.

The original church served the area until 1929. In this year the four acres on Toppenish Creek were exchanged for the two-and-one-half acres, where the present church now stands. The old building was torn down and the new one erected by an Indian crew. The new church was dedicated in 1930 by the most reverend R. J. Crimont, S.J., Bishop of Alaska. It was dedicated to Mary, our Sorrowful Mother on February 3, 1957.

Chapter 31

The Cathedral of Our Lady of Lourdes, Spokane, Washington, 1881

The Cathedral of Our Lady of Lourdes.

In August of 1881, Jesuit Father Joseph Cataldo converted a

carpenter's shop into the Church of St. Joseph, the first Catholic church in the Spokane Township. Like the smallest of seeds, the mustard seed, the Catholic faith had humble beginnings. Only five people attended the first mass in this wooden shed measuring 15 by 20 feet.

Five years later, a large brick church was dedicated to Our Lady of Loudes, replacing the original structure. The corner stone for the present church was laid in 1903. In 1913, the church became the cathedral for the newly created Diocese of Spokane.

In researching the early history of the spread of the gospel in the Northwest, the name of Father Joseph M. Cataldo, SJ. (1838-1928) is mentioned several times. He is often called the "Last of the Black Robes." He served the Coeur d'Alene, the Nez Perce, and other tribes in the Pacific Northwest as Superior of the Spokane-based Rocky Mountain Mission, placed on ministering to Native Americans. Cataldo's motto was "***Sumus primo pro Indianis***" ("Indians first").

Cataldo was born in Terrasaine, Sicily, March 17, 1837. He endured many childhood illnesses, nearly dying at the age of 2 and 5 years. At the age of 23, he was ordained as a priest at Leige, Belgium.

During his lifetime as a priest, Father Cataldo studied over 20 languages, including most European languages and the Native American languages of the Northwest. He was instrumental in the peace talks between Chief Joseph and General Howard following the Nez Perce Indian War of 1877.

Though he struggled with ill health most of his life, he lived to the age of 92. He died on April 8, 1928, at Pendleton, Oregon.

The front of the church

In "Chapter 3," we mentioned the European influence we observed in many churches in the Northwest.

This cathedral has many characteristics of European architecture but is facing north not east, as is the custom.

The cathedral is situated with its front doors facing north. The altar and the apse are facing south. The common practice of the Roman Catholic Church is the front facing the east.

Even when this is not possible as with this church, it is common practice to use terminology with regards to directions inside the church, as if the building was constructed facing the traditional direction. Thus, the altar is always described as sitting on the east end of the structure.

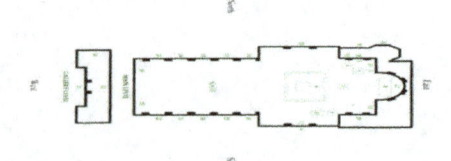

Chapter 32

Immaculate Conception Church, Roslyn, Washington, 1888

Immaculate Conception Catholic Church.

    The City of Roslyn is in central Washington, in the foothills of the Cascade Mountains. The city was named after Roslyn, NY, home of a coalminer's sweetheart. Two prospectors, Nez Jensen and George Verden, came looking for gold in 1886 and found a mountain of coal. When the Northern Pacific Railroad established the railroad across the mountains to Puget Sound, coal was needed for the steam locomotives, and the town of Roslyn was founded.

It did not take very long for Roslyn to become a typical mining town, with hundreds of hard-core coal miners who worked and played hard.

Saloons became the entertainment centers of the city and controlled the business section of the town. Between 1886 and 1929, workers came from many European countries to work in the mines. In 1891, Black coalminers were brought in to break a coalminers strike.

The Roslyn Cemetery has 26 individual ethnic cemeteries representing Italy, Poland, Germany, Lithuania, Slovenia, Scotland, England, Ireland, Serbia, and Croatia. In 1892, 45 men died in a coal mine explosion.

As with most settlements, the church was also very important in the life of the coal miners. It must have been around 1888 that the Immaculate Conception Church was constructed.

In many cases it was not feasible to hire a designer or architect, the best way was to get plans from another existing structure. It is not known if this was the case here.

The Church showing the cable anchors in the wall.

    This church was designed with buttresses to reinforce the stability of the high walls. Buttresses are placed on the outside of the building, thus eliminating pillars on the inside.

    From the beginning, the church showed some problems by starting to lean towards the south. In the 1950s, church leaders decided to "modernize" the structure by removing the buttresses that had been part of the original design.

    Concerns for the overall stability of the church came to a head in 2001. The Nisqually Quake caused the sanctuary to be closed for general worship.

    An estimated $250 would be needed for repairs. The rehabilitations were accomplished by a plan designed by the Rafn Co. of

Bellevue and Bainbridge Island architect Ron Lacey.

The curch with the new buttresses

The restoration of this building is another example of the fact that when a historic building needs repairs, it does not have to be taken down.

This church will be serving the community of believers for many more years and enhances the historic environment in the city of Roslyn.

A time of prayer is again enjoyed by the faithful.

Visiting the City of Roslyn, you will find history that is well preserved. From the historic buildings along main street to the unique cemeteries. You can imagine the activities around the saloons when this was a boom town.

The only item missing in all this is the sound of the steam locomotives, hauling coal and passengers to and from faraway places.

Serbian Cemetery photo with permission from Maggie Rail.

The buildings are over 100 years old, and were occupied by saloons, billiard halls, a barber shop, and wash houses. The churches remain the same; the Gospel is presented as it was many years ago.

Downtown Roslyn

Chapter 33

First Congregational Church, Coupeville Washington, 1889
St. Mary's Catholic Church, 1932

On January 17, 1866, Mrs. Daniel Pearson, accompanied by her teenage son and daughter, boarded the steamship Continental in New York to make the trip around the tip of South America to the Washington Territory. On May 31, they landed at Port Townend, the port of entry for the Washington Territory at that time. They would be part of the Second Mercer Expedition.

The first Mercer Expedition had sailed in 1864. Georgia and Josephine Pearson were members of that first group, they were called the "Mercer Girls," and they came to teach school. Both sisters had jobs on Whidbey Island. They were chaperoned by their father, who had secured a job as the lighthouse keeper there. He then sent for his wife and two teenagers.

The Pearson family and other pioneer families settled Central Whidbey Island and "land donations." Flora Pearson worked with her father as assistant lighthouse keeper for 11 years. On May 8, 1876, she was married to William B. Engle in Victoria, B.C. by Reverend A. Russ, a Wesleyan minister.

During the passing years, Flora A.P. Engle was actively teaching music to young people on the piano she had brought around the Horn on the ship from New York. She was also active in helping to organize the Congregational Christian group in the 1880s. It was brought together officially on Sunday, February 20, 1887, in the Methodist Church in Coupeville. The first business meeting of the Congregational Church was held in the Puget Sound Academy;

but services were held on the alternating Sundays at the Methodist Church.

In June 1889, the building of the Church began on property given by the Puget Sound Academy. By October 5, 1889, the congregation was meeting at their new church.

In the year 1890, they received a bell for the church from the McShane Bell Foundry of Baltimore, Maryland. The total weight was 800 pounds and was made of bell metal—i.e. 80% copper, 20 % tin, and cost $205. It was a gift to the church and was inscribed as follows:

> *"O Come, Let Us Worship"*
> *Presented to the*
> *First Congregational Church, Coupeville*
> *by T.W. Calhoon & E.J. Hancock*
> *1890.*

In June 1900, after much discussion and postponing, Rev. Newberry himself painted the church, returning $27.55 of the allotted paint money to the treasurer. The parishioners voted to give this money to their much beloved pastor as "salary."

In 1913, they found it necessary to remove the tall spire and build a lower tower that would be easier to maintain. The rebuilt steeple was completed in 1917.

The year 1928 found the church membership declining due to the younger people moving off the island, and the older members, many original founders, passing to their reward. It was noted that a cord of wood cost $4.00. Also, it was found necessary to place a lighted electric bulb inside the piano to keep it dry.

In December 1939, the Congregational Community met once more to discuss selling the church to the Catholics. It was not until June 1934 that the building was sold for $1500. This money was used to pay $350 to the Congregational Church board to close out the mortgage on the church. All other debts were paid.

Chapter 34
Holy Trinity Episcopal Church, Wallace Idaho, 1910

Holy Trinity Episcopal Church

    This church was built to replace the 1889 wooden structure at the same location. Historic Wallace was destroyed by fire on July 27, 1890, only two structures survived. The surrounding forests were also spared. This time predominantly masonry structures were built for better fire resistance. The city is now on the national but services were held on the alternating Sundays at the Methodist Church.

In June 1889, the building of the Church began on property given by the Puget Sound Academy. By October 5, 1889, the congregation was meeting at their new church.

In the year 1890, they received a bell for the church from the McShane Bell Foundry of Baltimore, Maryland. The total weight was 800 pounds and was made of bell metal—i.e. 80% copper, 20 % tin, and cost $205. It was a gift to the church and was inscribed as follows:

"O Come, Let Us Worship"
Presented to the
First Congregational Church, Coupeville
by T.W. Calhoon & E.J. Hancock
1890.

In June 1900, after much discussion and postponing, Rev. Newberry himself painted the church, returning $27.55 of the allotted paint money to the treasurer. The parishioners voted to give this money to their much beloved pastor as "salary."

In 1913, they found it necessary to remove the tall spire and build a lower tower that would be easier to maintain. The rebuilt steeple was completed in 1917.

The year 1928 found the church membership declining due to the younger people moving off the island, and the older members, many original founders, passing to their reward. It was noted that a cord of wood cost $4.00. Also, it was found necessary to place a lighted electric bulb inside the piano to keep it dry.

In December 1939, the Congregational Community met once more to discuss selling the church to the Catholics. It was not until June 1934 that the building was sold for $1500. This money was used to pay $350 to the Congregational Church board to close out the mortgage on the church. All other debts were paid.

Chapter 34

Holy Trinity Episcopal Church, Wallace Idaho, 1910

Holy Trinity Episcopal Church

    This church was built to replace the 1889 wooden structure at the same location. Historic Wallace was destroyed by fire on July 27, 1890, only two structures survived. The surrounding forests were also spared. This time predominantly masonry structures were built for better fire resistance. The city is now on the national

Register of Historic Places.

The Holy Trinity Episcopal church is one of the few churches designed by an architect just for one particular location. Most churches constructed on or before 1900 were copies of other churches constructed in the eastern part of the country. It was a common practice to pass the blueprints around to different congregations in the same denomination.

This church was designed by the famous designer Kirtland K. Cutter who was the designer of several buildings in Spokane Falls. The Davenport Hotel and the Spokane Chronicle building are some of the buildings. Mr. Cutter was born in Cleveland, Ohio, on the 20th of August 1860. He was educated at the Brooks Military Academy. For five years, he studied art and architecture in the principal cities of America and Europe.

In 1886, he came to Spokane Falls and worked for the First National Bank for one year before he established himself as an architect. Downtown Spokane reflects the brilliance of this architect in many buildings not designed but influenced by Mr. Cutter.

The design of this building is similar to a building in Santa Cruz County, Arizona. It is not known if Mr. Cutter saw this structure, but there is a resemblance in design, and burned brick was also used in parts of this structure.

Protruding burned brick design is unique to this structure. The top of the square corner tower blew off in a strong wind and had to be capped. The corner buttresses give stability to the tower.

In the fall of 1889, Bishop Talbot arrived in the mining camp of Wallace. His mission was to hold church services in George and Human's Hall. The meeting consisted mostly of men, although the lady's guild was established in 1888. He was successful in collecting $1500 to buy an $80 lot, as well as building materials. On August 20, 1902, the congregation organized and became the first parish in the state of Idaho. By 1910, the old church became too small for the congregation, and the new church was constructed.

The Mission in Santa Cruz Arizona

This area in the State of Idaho, known as the Coeur d'Alene Mining region, is famous for the mining of silver, gold, zinc, lead, and copper.

The area is roughly four miles wide and twenty miles long and ranked first in the annual production of silver being mined for several years.

Chapter 35

Mount Pisgah Presbyterian Church, Roslyn Washington, 1886

Information supplied by Marjorie Hathaway from the church archives.

The moment Pisgah church

It was on October 10, 1885, when Rev. Isam Wheelis was commissioned by the Board of Home Missions of the Presbyterian Church to labor in the Teanaway and Wenatchee Valleys. After a thorough exploration of the field, he found it impractical to connect the two valleys under one minister owing to the distance between them and the high range of hills which are covered with snow until late in the spring.

He began his labors in the Teanaway country on October 25, 1885, with the purpose of organizing a Presbyterian Church. On

March 28, 1886, after a discourse by Rev. J.A. Laurie from Matthew 14:13-21 about the feeding of the 5000. The MT. Pisgah Presbyterian Church was organized.

The name Mount Pisgah is the name of the mountain Moses was led to by the Lord to show him the promised land before he died.

The session and trustees then held a joint meeting when a contract was entered into with Rev. I. Wheelis to become their supply pastor for the term of one year, pledging him $1,000.00 per year.

Services were held in the schoolhouse in the un-incorporated village of Teanaway, Kittitas County, Washington Territory on March 28, 1886. On June 29, 1886, the town of Roslyn was located and named by Logan M. Bullet, and in August 1886, Cle Elum was located and named by Walter Read and Thos. Johnson.

At the March 28, 1899, congregational meeting a motion was made to build a new church. Two committees were appointed, one to solicit funds and one to find a location to build. The church was constructed by March 26, 1900, at a cost of $3,840.64.

A beautiful reed organ was installed. The organ is a reed organ not a pipe organ, the pipes showing are ornamental only. The air required to operate the organ is supplied with an electric motor. When it was first installed, the air was supplied mechanically from the basement with bellows.

The reed organ

    The organ was made by the Clough & Warren Organ Co. The company started in 1850 in Detroit, Michigan, under the name of W.P. Blakeman

    After several name changes, it came to be known as the Clough & Warren Co. of Adrian Michigan in 1874. The company went bankrupt in 1911, reorganized in 1913, and discontinued organ production in 1916. The Reed Organ Society, Inc. was founded in 1981, and is devoted to the appreciation, study, collection, and restoration of reed organs.

    In most churches the reed organs are now replaced by the new electronic keyboards and pianos. This organ is now used for special occasions only.

    It appears that the original design of this church was typical European with a large open sanctuary, and the area of the chancel is designed with a rounded back wall. The chancel is the area where the pulpit and the choir are located.

    The main entry way is at the front of the building.

    At the January 25, 1904, meeting, it was voted to put a partition to divide that auditorium and move the pulpit to the end of the auditorium next to the Manse.

The rounded back part of the church building.

(The Manse is the name given to the home of the pastor; other denominations call this the Parsonage.)

Inside the sanctuary

This change located the main entry way to the side of the building.

The congregation was served by several pastors. From 1885 until today, 49 pastors are listed. This is typical to all the early churches. Serving under difficult conditions and in most cases for very low wages. It was recorded that in 1952, the pastor's salary was raised to $100 per month.

In 1890, the Synodical Missionary, Rev. Thomas M. Gunn, D.D. reported that he had been in Roslyn in November-December. The following is a comment he made about the pastor:

"To my dismay the young man as partially insane and much of my time for several weeks was occupied in caring for him and in securing his safe return to his friends."

We must keep in mind that Roslyn was a coalmining town. Life was not easy for believers in such an environment and was extremely difficult for the ministers of the Gospel.

Chapter 36

Seventh - Day Adventists Church, Walla Walla, Washington, 1874

First Adventist Church in the Northwest Walla Walla Washington 1874.

Information from "A Journey Through Time" by Doug R. Johnson (with permission).

    Unlike most parts of the United States, Adventism entered the Inland Northwest when it was a lightly populated frontier. When Augusta Moorhouse, the first Adventist in the Pacific Northwest, crossed the Oregon trail with her family and settled in the remote Walla Walla Valley, only 12,000 people were living in the Washington Territory. When the first Adventist minister, Isaac Van Horn, arrived in 1874, the territory was still unsettled with a population of only 50,000.

    A small group of Adventist settled in the Walla Walla valley in the late 1860s. They requested a minister from the General Conference, but the denominational leaders could not spare one of their few ministers for a remote area such as the Northwest.

It would be six years after their first request for help that Isaac and Adelia Van Horn would travel to the Northwest and launch their ministry in the beautiful Walla Walla Valley.

Van Horn started by holding evangelistic meetings in his 60-foot tent, which attracted large crowds each evening. By the end of the year, he was able to organize a church of 60 members, who erected one of the nicest buildings in the region. Van Horn also baptized Alonzo T. Jones, who was a soldier at Fort Walla Walla. The next year, Jones began working as Van Horn's assistant.

The sleepy Pacific Northwest woke up in the 1880's to the sound of the train whistle. In 1883, the Northern Pacific Railroad completed it transcontinental line and connected the Inland Northwest to the rest of the nation with a safe and rapid form of transportation. The results were amazing. The population of the Washington Territory went from 75,000 in 1880 to 357,000 in 1890.

Unfortunately, Adventism was not prepared for this transformation of the region. Instead, strong-willed and independent-minded members along with some unstable, new ministers forced the leaders to focus on damage control and the handling of internal problems.

The church in Zillah Washington

Finally, in 1884, Ellen White and six ministers from California traveled to the Northwest to meet the situation. Ellen White described the crisis as "one of the hardest battles we ever had to engage in."

The result of this meeting was a refocus on the mission instead of the problems. The church experienced a rapid growth in the area, starting in Spokane Falls, Moscow, Boise City, Farmington, and all through the eastern part of the state.

In the city of Zillah, the church purchased a beautiful building that was constructed in 1910 by the Church of Christ.

This is a perfect way to preserve the historic buildings. When a denomination has no use for a building for worship to sell it to another.

As we are living in a throw-away society, it is refreshing to see the building preserved.

Chapter 37

Old St. Peter's Episcopal Church, Tacoma, Washington, 1873

Information from the official church website, with permission.

The Old St. Peter's Church

    Old St. Peter's Church was built in 1873 at the behest of the Right Reverend Benjamin Wister Morris, the Protestant Episcopal Bishop of the diocese of Oregon and of Washington Territory.

    E.S. Smith donated the land; George Atkinson provided the motivation; the Hanson and Ackerson Mill provided the timber; and the townsmen built the church in record time.

    Through an oddity of law, Bishop Morris discovered that he, and not the diocese, owned the church building, and in 1907, he conveyed the property to the new Missionary Diocese of Washington.

Between 1873 and 1907, St. Peter's followed the canon law of the local Episcopal Church diocese even though a majority of the congregation's governing board during those years was often not Episcopalian.

On most occasions, worship services were conducted by layman or by visiting clergy of diverse denominational callings, whose communions were not always given to mutual forbearance and Christian charity.

Old St. Peter's before the turn of the century
Photo courtesy of the Washington State Historical Society

The bell tower circa 1874 is a cut-off tree well over 300 years old, encouraging the statement like, "The Oldest Bell Tower in North America."

The bottom of the bell tower and the root of the ivy.

Note the cross on the bell tower is facing toward the bay to invite the seafaring shipmates to attend worship. Now it is facing the community.

The bell tower is covered with ivy, and the bell is now rung from the inside of the building.

The ivy must be trimmed back so it will not interfere with the ringing of the bell.

The sanctuary with the wood stove and pump organ.

This sanctuary is in the most original condition that we have seen in our research of historic churches. The woodstove on the left is not being used today but is in its original location. The ceiling shows the location of the vents that were used to let the smoke out when it got too bad for the worshippers.

The organ came around Cape Horn in 1874 as part of the private baggage of an immigrant family. Fares in those days were not fixed, and the cost of transportation could escalate if bad winds or medical emergencies slowed the ship. In this case, the family had to sell some of their furniture at auction on the dock to satisfy their debt to the ship's captain. There was no real money in Tacoma then, so a note for $150 with St. Peter's as the debtor was given in exchange for the organ which was dragged up the hill.

The church now had an instrument and Anna Wolfe, a young woman of the Hebrew faith, became the organist until 1886. Giving recitals, teaching music, and donating the proceeds to the church, she paid off the note in three years. She also paid off the $300 note from the mill for the lumber to build the church in 1873.

Among the many saints of God, Ana Wolfe reminds us of the meaning of sacrifice.

Chapter 38

Bethel African Methodist Episcopal Church, Yakima Washington, 1906

Information from the hundredth anniversary book and the official web site.

The church building.

    The African Methodist Episcopal Church grew out of the Free African Society which Richard Allen, Absalom Jones, and others established in Philadelphia in 1787. When officials at St. George's church pulled blacks off their knees while praying, FAS members discovered just how far American Methodist would go to enforce racial discrimination against African Americans.

    The members of St. George's made plans to change their mutual aid society into an African congregation. Most of them wanted to affiliate with the Protestant Episcopal Church, but Allen led a small group who resolved to remain Methodist.

In 1794, Bethel AME was dedicated with Allen as pastor. To establish Bethel's independence from interfering white Methodists, Allen, a former Delaware slave, successfully sued in the Pennsylvania courts in 1807 and in 1815 for the right of his congregation to exist as an independent institution.

The geographical spread of the AMEC prior to the Civil War was mainly restricted to the Northeast and Midwest. Remarkably, the slave states of Maryland, Kentucky, Missouri, Louisiana, and, for a few years, South Carolina, became additional locations for the AME congregations.

The denomination reached the Pacific Coast in the early 1850s. The church in Yakima Washington was established in December 1906. From 1906 to 1917, under the administration of Rev. S.E. Baily, the embers of Bethel Church met in rooms over the Bragg's Barber Shop.

The interiior of the church.

On January 19, 1919, the Articles of Incorporation were filed with the County Auditor, and on May 22, 1910, the cornerstone of the Bethel AME Church was in progress. 25 years later, on May 22, 1935, Dr. John Coleman and the Rev. W. Sims conducted the services at the dedication of Bethel African Methodist Church building on the corner of South Sixth and Beech Streets.

Many of Bethel's members have passed on, but Bethel African Methodist Episcopal Church continues to grow in unity, serving the Yakima Southeast Community faithfully and spiritually.

The closeness of this community was recorded in the following from the souvenir book:

> **Uncle Morris as known to us all, left us in a blazing flash and glory with pomp and circumstance. He marched out from the one place he considered home and that was here in the church using neither wheelchair or crutches. His escort came during the altar call on the Day of Ascension. With the choir singing his favorite hymn, "Yes God is real," he sung a few words, "for I can feel Him in my soul," then he slipped into the arms of Jesus.**

Mother's Story

Our mother was a great storyteller, and she would tell us stories from her childhood that we have never forgotten. She would say, "Life is liked a vapor." This story illustrates that: just before midnight on Old Year's Eve, in the village where she lived, the people would leave their homes and go to the church in the center of town. The sound of wooden shoes on the cobble stone streets could be heard coming from all directions. At exactly midnight, the church bell would ring twelve times. As they gathered outside the church, the Pastor would lead them in singing the following hymn:

Hours and days, and years and ages
Swift as moving shadows flee:
As we scan life's fleeting pages
Naught enduring do we see:
On the path our feet are wending
Footprints all will be ef-faced;
Present time to past is tending,
Tough its page is not erased.

Manuscript. Herrnhut Choralbuch 1735
Translation from Dutch Hymn by Rev. L.P. Brink, 1929.